ESCAPE
IMPOSSIBLE

(The crime and punishment story of corrupt
politicians)

BOOK –ONE

INCIDENT -1

The time was 11.30 am; that was a day before the Deepavali-the entire Chennai city was overexcited over buying and selling clothes, crackers, sweets etc. There was traffic congestion everywhere on the city roads. With the available police force, it was a mockery of sort for controlling the mad crowd of vehicles and the pedestrian population bursting on the seams.

The Old Mahabalipuram Road was not an exception. It had its quota of traffic snarls even on normal days and the eve of the Deepavali festival, the vehicles are waiting for signals on all four sides of the junction at the SHolinganallur. The signals as usual bungled and the two police men –one in uniform and the other in plain clothes were apologies for traffic controlling force.

When there was a change over from one side to another- when the policeman was showing the stop board, a big bodied Innova car rushed out to turn to the right side of the road, hit an auto which was coming from the left side as per the signal of the policeman. Right under the eyes of all those who were waiting in all sorts of vehicles, the auto made a somersault and dashed against the road divider with a loud noise and the right side of the car receiving the impact of the collision, spewed glass pieces from the right side head lights, besides a big dent on the bonnet and the front right side door.

It all happened within a fraction of a second. But what followed was a nightmare. The person who got down from the car happened to a sitting ruling party MLA and fortunately, there were no passengers in the auto but the auto driver also escaped with minor injuries. But the accident resulted in a major damage to the auto.

2

The MLA started abusing the policeman and his bodyguard-likes started taking the auto driver into task while the public witnessing the scene started shouting at the MLA and charged him as the cause for the accident. The crowd at the junction started going beyond the control of the two poor constables and they promptly contacted their higher-ups and were trying to do their best to bring everything under control.

MLA phoned up and summoned further support as things were going against him and many auto drivers were joining the affected auto man and a stage for free for all clash was imminent.

At that a time, a scooter rider who was watching the whole incident from the front row – put the stand for his vehicle and pushed aside those surrounding the MLA and confronted him directly.

"Sir, please look at me and tell – whether or not your driver committed the mistake which resulted in the accident?"

The whole crowd suddenly kept quiet and there ensued a strange silence in the area which was seconds before wearing a riotous look.

After a few minutes looking here and there, the MLA quietly said-" i think my driver was wrong"

On hearing the MLA owning the mistake the public present were shouting excitedly raising their hands as if they had won some battle.

The scooter man then asked the MLA " thank you sir, you have accepted your mistake like a brave man. Are you ready to compensate the auto driver for the damage you have caused?"

Again there was a pause- " I can provided – he should not ask whatever comes to his mind"

Then the scooter man called the affected auto driver who emerged with his fellow auto gang and was looking like a caged tiger-fretting and fuming.

"The MLA has accepted the mistake and is ready to pay for the damage. You can include the loss of daily net income for the days which would required for setting right the vehicle. But your demand should be fair and reasonable"

There was a sudden change in the behaviour of auto driver who immediately went into discussions with his fellow drivers. After a few

3

minutes, he said that at least fifteen thousand was required to cover up the loss due to accident.

The scooter man asked the driver," look at me and tell me the correct amount ".

The driver looked sheepishly for a few seconds and said, " at least i want eight thousand – five for the repair and three as the income last for five days."

The scooter-man then turned towards the MLA and asked him whether it was acceptable to him.

Instead of replying the MLA opened the car and within a few minutes got the eight thousand demanded by the auto and was trying to give to the scooter-man who politely refused to take it but requested the MLA to hand it over to the affected party.

Within ten minutes the deal was over . Both the MLA and the auto driver thanked the scooter man and the people who were witnessing the whole episode were flabbergasted by the speed at which a possible serious clash was amicable settled by a lone scooter man who sprang up from nowhere to achieve peace and peaceful flow of traffic.

Within the next thirty minutes the traffic congestion was eased . By the time the higher-ups turned to the spot of problem with additional reinforcement of traffic constables, the traffic was moving normally and there was not a semblance of an accident at the junction except the strewn glass pieces from the car head lights.

People thanked the scooter man who was looking bewildered and shocked as to how a timid person like him under normal circumstances could complete a peaceful deal casually – stopping the bloodshed ,unwanted litigation and serious public inconvenience due to traffic block.

When he told his wife and parents after reaching home – no one believed him till they saw his face and how he handled the issue through the TVs and the next day news papers. Overnight he became a hero and had to meet the press often and repeat the same thing again and again-which no one believed

" i do not know what happened to me. I was waiting for the signal. Suddenly i felt that i should go and talk to the MLA and others . That is all i knew and how i handled the matter and how i talked and why the MLA agreed to my request were all not because of me and my talents. I think that some unknown thing made me to do what i had done yesterday at the accident site."

But no one believed him and he was in the lime light for a few days before other hot news eclipsed the Sholinganallur Junction incident.

INCIDENT -2

The Court at the District Headquarters started as usual at 10 am. There were many cases posted for that day and the crowd gathered in and around the court premises within and outside the compound, included the lawyers, their juniors, witnesses, the relatives of the accused or defendants, police personnel escorting the alleged criminals re be physically present during the hearings, besides some reporters of media. Every one present was looking busy expressing all kinds of emotions-depending upon their expectations from the hearings at the assigned courts.

In front of the entrance to some of the court halls- eleven to be exact- there were more people than some of the court halls which almost looked deserted at 10 am.

But the court No three was wearing a special look on that day- an ex-minister was going to be present in a land grab case deploying force and personal influence. The people gathered were eagerly waiting for the ex to arrive and presently the judges took over their seats and the first case for the day was taken up as per protocol.

After fifteen minutes when the first two cases were adjourned to another suitable dates either for the defendant or the plaintiff, the number of the case of the Minister was announced by the court peon. Just then from nowhere the minister emerged among the crowd escorted by a posse of police personnel. The ex- Minister bowed before the judges and took the stand for the defendant.

The case details were read out. The defendant lawyer stood up and started placing his appeal for bail for his client explaining various reasons which included the proposed marriage of the ex-minister's second daughter within a month.

The government pleader thereafter filed his petitions for objections to the bail besides explaining why the defendant should not be given the bail at that junction of the investigation and filing of the final charge sheet.

There were some heated arguments and counter arguments when suddenly – one of the juniors of the government pleader stood up and

5

asked for the permission of the judges to examine the defendant not on behalf of the government but on behalf of the general public.

There were some visible commotions among the people gathered there in the court gallery and also among the lawyers of the defendant as well as among the government pleaders. The presiding single judge took a few minutes to decide and finally he allowed the junior lawyer to cross examine the defendant but within the scope of the case only and also with a severe warning that if he (junior) did not justify his special request and appeared to have wasted the time of the court proceedings, he would be taken into task through the bar council forthwith.

The junior bowed and thanked the judge while accepting the stringent condition of the sanction to examine the defendant.
He then went around the long table of lawyers and stood before the ex-minister and asked the defendant-

" Sir, you were a minister in three cabinets in the past and were the sitting MLA for six times. Now look at me and tell the court that you have not committed any crime in taking possession of the land belonging to the plaintiff –Damodara Mudaliar ?

There was a shocking silence that prevailed for a few seconds but just then the defendant lawyer stood up and objected to the question of the junior on the ground that the case was relating to the bail application and there was no charge sheet as yet from the police or from government and as such the junior had violated the condition of the sanction of the honourable court and wasted the invaluable time of the court.

There was loud appreciation from the gallery since those who were present –were belonging to the supporters of the ex-minister and his stooges.

The judge was also irritated to the extent of shouting at the junior that he had misused his sanction .

At that point, the defendant the ex-minister politely folded his hands to show his respect to the judge and said,

" Your honour- please do not mistake this young lawyer. He asked the question whether i have committed any offence in buying the land." He then looked around at those who were present which included the reporters of the media and with his patented beaming smile- after adjusting his towel over his shoulders –and continued to tell,

"your honour- yes- i admit – i have used force to make the Mudaliar to sell the land to me. That three acres of land was badly required for my son who was constructing a hotel in the town. We were requesting the plaintiff to quote any rate he wanted but he was not listening and refused to sell the land. Hence, i had to use the force – i sent a car load of my friends to persuade him to complete the sale and within 24 hours we registered the sale in my son's favour. But a mistake happened without my knowledge and instruction. The visiting team of friends to the Mudaliar misbehaved with the daughter of the plaintiff and hurt the son and a few others present in the house at that time. That information was not conveyed to me then and there. But when i came to know of it, i went to meet the Mudaliar to regret but the man was behaving like a wounded tiger and started attacking me, even without giving a chance to explain. Finally the purpose of my visit was lost and Mudaliar himself was beaten right under my nose and with my permission. Of course, the police played their usual game. Before the affected people could file a case against me and my men, we went to meet commissioner and filed a case against the Mudaliar after i cut myself deliberately on my arms and thighs- the safe places. With the bleeding injuries i appeared before the press people and earned notorious publicity for the offence i committed. What followed was simple- Mudaliar was arrested with his sons and their men- and released on bail subsequently at my request. Now after the change of the government, i find the case was once again filed against me and others by Mudaliar. Poor fellow- he was put into torture and mental tension over these two years.

Your honour- whatever i have said was true and no one compelled me to tell what i have told. But i do not want my son to be brought into this case nor my men who obeyed my orders only in attacking the plaintiff and his family members"

The Ex-Minister spoke like a warrior- defeated by looking proud. The gallery stood up speechless and the defendant lawyers bowed down their heads as a mark of disgrace for them in taking a case for the ex-minister foolishly. The press people were going amuck in shooting the beaming ex-minster and the excited family members of the Mudaliar. But Mudaliar himself could not be present as he was undergoing treatment for his sickness which had compelled him to be bedridden.

The judge slammed the wooden hammer and said " this case is adjourned. The date and timing would be announced by the court registrar. Now, Mr Junior, i am sorry to have shouted at you. What this court and the system of judiciary would not be able to achieve in the normal course, you have done it within a minute and that too, by asking only one question. Hats off to you, young man" the judge bowed before the junior and stepped down from the platform on his way to his chamber.

The Minister was whisked away by the police in a hurry after the judge left and the ex-minster party also followed the minister to the waiting police van. The court hall was left with the plaintiff family and the government pleader and his assistants – the press reporters, a few members of the public- and of course the hero- the junior pleader grade 4- Ramasamy.

Everyone congratulated Ramasamy and he became an instant celebrity in that place. But he was repeatedly telling everyone who came to wish him-

" please listen to me- i do not deserve the praise for making the Ex-minister to tell the truth on his own. I was like you all watching the proceedings of the case when i felt that i should go and talk to the defendant. What made to do that, i do not know. But i am sure that it has nothing to do with my question and further, till i asked the question, i did not have the faintest idea that the ex-minister would blurt out the truth just like that - upon my simple request. It was strange and not within my powers to make a person to tell the truth. Something forced to me to do what I have done"-
But no one listened to him and he hit the headlines of all the media and even his parents and relatives did not believe what he said about the external influence which was responsible for the unexpected confession of the minister.

INCIDENT-3

The traffic was stopped for a few minutes. There were loud reports from the cracker-bombs somewhere from a bye-lane . The thousands of devotees thronged that small road waiting for their spiritual gurus to arrive at- for attending the Mahaygna performed for World peace at Chennai – in that the Island grounds- the biggest open space in Chennai city- which could accommodate at least 50000 persons . The top spiritual leaders all over the world have agreed to be present at the last day of the Yagna while the yahna was performed by His Holiness Swami Swarganandaji the founder of a new religious body called Moksha Peetam. It was his first appearance in the Tamilnadu. Within three years of establishing the peedam, at Maharashtra - Swamiji became the most sought after holy man in the country because of his reported magical powers of curing illness at the last stage, childless getting children, half blind becoming normal besides poor getting financial help which they could not even imagine.

One after another the Babas, Swamijis, Adigalars, gurumaharajs, etc were arriving in tight security with their band of disciples and close followers and body guards. The devotees attached to those holy men were assembling in that biggest open area in Tamil nadu in thousands. The yagna was being performed for the past ten days and that was the last day when the ritual would be completed as per the holy rules. His Holiness Swami Swargaanandaji was the last to arrive at 11 am- though the program for that day already commenced at 6 am and almost all the invitees had come and were given warm welcome and were seated at a special gallery provided with all the comforts. Amidst the cracker sounds- and devotees cries of long life for him, an elephant garlanded the host swamiji and a team of prohits chanting mantras were garlanding him, throwing flowers over his head and finally he was requested to stop when they started washing his foot with holy water mixed with turmeric powder and kunkum etc. He was shown burning camphor deepa aradhana and the simple looking holy person entered the yagna hall - surrounded by hundreds of VVIP and VIP devotees, all over the world which included top industrialists and cine actors and cricket players besides Chief Ministers , MLAs, MPs and central and state ministers- except perhaps the PM and the President because PM was on an international tour and President was indisposed. They were reported to have given a message to the press expressing their regret to have missed such a rare occasion and an event for world peace.

At the specially decorated raised platform - a glittering throne was ready for the Swamiji to sit along with other senior spiritual greats like him who were also sitting on similar thrones but the host was in the centre of the holy group – just to show that he was running the show.

The yagna was nearing its end and the hundreds of prohits who were chanting the mantras for ten days continuously in turn were looking exhausted and worn out due to the fumes coming out from the fire burning non-stop for ten days. Around 11.30 am Swamiji Swargananda got up from his throne and all other holy men also stood up . They all marched towards the 21 yagna pits where the holy pooja was being performed. The prohits politely handed over a bag of something which the swaminji and the other holy persons dropped over the fire pit. That was the ultimate ritual to mark the end of the yagna when the whole area was ripped with cracker bombs and bell sounds besides the shouting of long live peace for the world by nearly sixty thousand people gathered there in that open ground partially covered by thatched roofs of dry coconut leaves .

The next item in the agenda of the program of the final day was the address by each one of the spiritual leaders. Accordingly the holy men started addressing the crowd and those who were the devotees of the person addressing would stand up and shout 'long live' wishes for their spiritual guru.

After two lesser known religious leaders in Tamil Nadu spoke briefly for a few minutes in Hindi-translated in Tamil simultaneously, the third speaker stood up to proceed to podium to start his felicitation, a lone voice from the people sitting in front of the platform stopped the proceeding abruptly A tall person wearing dhoti was standing with his raised hand- telling something to the holy group. All the heads of the VVIPs, VIPs and others turned towards that person, when the swamiji swargananada took the mike and asked that person to come to the stage.

Pushing people here and there, that thin-looking old man reached the platform. He bowed before the holy group when the leader of the function asked him to tell what he wanted to say a few minutes before.

" My pranams to you and other holy ones here. I do not know whether i have the right or whether it is right to ask a question to all of you in the presence of ministers, MLAs, MPs, big businessmen and the public besides the media " the old man was blurting in broken words looking here and there and scanning over the crowd of devotees who were showing irritation on their faces due to the impertinent intrusion of the stranger among the holy group.

Swarga anada simply smiled showing divinity all over his person- " my dear sir, this is a divine function. Here all are equal and if you have something to ask, you can ask us. Among the thousands present before us, only you have boldly stood up to ask. Go ahead and ask whatever you want to and we will tell what we know without hesitation. But pleas be brief and to the point and do not hurt the sentiments of the people present here or criticize this yagna and our faith please"

He then looked around the gathering with a beaming smile to show as to how he was a true benevolent spiritual guru and as expected, the devotees were shedding tears of respect and were reacting visibly to show that they were terribly impressed by the generous action of their guru.

The TVs were showing the program live all over India and they focussed their cameras on the holy group, the devotees, and lastly on the lone emaciated looking person looking timid and stage shy.

"Sir i thank you . Now can i start from the beginning- that is- can i start from the two holiness who have already addressed ?" the old man was asking nervously. The swamiji without answering the old man but requested the two to come forward one by one and clear the doubts of the old man.

The first one stood up from his seat and commanded the old man to shoot the question.

" are you really a holy person as you claim or are you an ordinary person with all the weakness of a common man?"

The cracker-bombs noise if heard from a ten feet distance would not have made that much impact on those who were present on that big thatched temporary hall.

"Boo-boos- get outs, throw that fellow etc" started instantly from the hundreds of devotees shouting and waving their hands asking the old man to get out or face the consequences in all languages. The swamji Swargananda himself was taken aback and never expected a question of that seriousness and madness from that old man and the same case with other holy men present.

The VVIPs and VIPs present gave instructions to the top police officials to remove the black sheep then and there and show him the police treatment.

It took some ten minutes for the commotion to subside when policemen rushed to the platform to whisk away the mad old man when the swamiji to whom the question was asked – stopped the policemen and asked them to keep away from the old man.

" i request all of you to show restrain. The asker of the question needs an answer because today we have hundreds of people calling themselves god men and messenger of god or avathara purushas etc. People like the old man here are millions in the country but they have no guts to ask the holy persons whether they are really holy or wholly or empty.

On my part, i would like to declare that i am an ordinary person. I do not do any magic or miracle. I belong to a backward class in Madhya Pradesh – a remote village . I am not educated. But in my village there was a village medical man- their families for generations were doctors for the villages. I once-became sick and was treated by the village doctor. I was impressed by the way in which the treatment was given to me. I asked the doctor whether i could also learn the art of curing sick people. He was around seventy plus at that time and was issueless, besides his wife had died long back. He agreed and taught me the nuances of native medicine and told me that still certain herbs were there in high mountains which could cure some serious illnesses which not even the educated doctors could cure in big hospitals in the cities . But he had not made any attempts to get the herbs as he was not interested in leaving the village to migrate to the nearby towns to practice there to earn more. Further he added that he had no one as his dependent and what he had earned and kept at the village was sufficient for him till his death.

I went in search of the herbs and after strenuous efforts over two years i found them and slowly i developed medicines for serious illnesses and settled down in Bhopal. But what made me not to call me as a native medicine doctor i did not know. I started simply giving medicines, for a token small fees, for the poor people   who approached me. When my medicines worked wonders, within five years i became very famous in Madhya Pradesh. I stopped receiving even the token fees and in return i received money, jewels and other values in plenty as gifts by the patients who became my devotees. Thus I was accepted as person with divine power. Now and then i would disappear to the mountains under the pretext of meditation, to procure the rare herbs and back again in Bhopal the people would wait for days to have my darshan or appointment .

That was my story of holiness. I have not been enlightened like Buddha or the Sankaracharaya. I am a simple herbal doctor. Actually only the herbs are holy ones which could cure even cancer in the initial stages. "

He then looked at the old man and said –" sir i have replied to your questions. But for the second question whether i have the weaknesses of an ordinary person, i would like to assure you that i have no sexual interest or to make money to live luxuriously. I have not cheated any one so far. The name and fame all came to me on their own. I am quite comfortable

11

and happy with the wealth the herbs got me as holy man and not for the herbal treatment"

He sat down and gave the mike to the next hold man who already addressed the crowd , who hesitated but the old man said-" sir look at me and tell whether or not you are willing to reply to my questions?" There was a look of confusion on the face of the second holy man. After shaking his head this side and that side- he took the mike and said-

" i admit i am not a holy man and have all the weaknesses of an ordinary person. I used lot of magic and stage managed miracles back in native place in Karnataka, in the beginning. People believed whatever i did and called me a divine person. I have crores of rupees worth landed assets besides cash and jewellery. Many political bigwigs and cine fames are my disciples." He completed his brief confession and sheepishly sat down in a corner of big throne. He did not know to whom the mike was to be given next when the old man looked at the Swami Swargananadaji. It lasted for a few seconds when the swamiji moved out from his throne and took the mike to reply –out of turn -to the questions of the old man .

"Sir, whoever you are- i am ashamed to call myself a holy person. Like the swamiji who learned the power of rare herbs, i learnt the power of witchcraft and hypnotism from a sadhu at Himalayas where i was earning as a guide in the holy town of Rishikesh- i was married and have two children- but the income was barely sufficient for running the family, when the stroke of luck made unexpected changes in my life in the form of two persons who came in search of a sadhu who was reported to be a top class witchcraft practitioner according to those who came in search of that sadhu. I was a native of Rishikesh but i did not know of the sadhu. With the three of us which included a native like me – it took two days to locate the sadhu- a native Keralite- settled down on the Ganges banks years back . He was living in a small hut cooking and looking after himself alone.

He was surprised to see the three of us and asked how they knew that he was there for away from the mad world of selfish people. Despite repeated requests and finally threatening by the two, the sadhu refused to oblige them to harm some distant enemies of the two in business. When things took a nasty turn the sadhu told them flatly- " if you two do leave north India within next 24 hours i will curse you with all the strength of my witchcraft skills ". The two took to their heels and in-between i became a devotee of the sadhu. I was frequently visiting him offering the food prepared by my wife and slowly i entered in his good books. It was possible because of the natural gift of my marketing and communication skills- but i could not succeed with those skills to earn what i wanted from working as a freelance guide.

One day when i found the sadhu was laid with fever and was very weak, i told him story of sufferings and how i needed money badly to make a decent living. He was moved by the way i told my suffering of course exaggerated to the extent required. It took two months for him to teach me first the witchcraft. He then handed over a bundle of old Palmyra leaves containing the mantras which could spell disaster for the people targeted. In addition to the witchcraft he taught me hypnotism as a bonus for one month. In return for his services he took a promise from me that i would perform the last rites after his death as per his religion- a Keralite Hindu Namboodri.

He lived for a few more months when i attended to all his needs including food and medicine and he died peacefully in sleep. I performed his last rites as desired by him on the Ganges banks and thereafter migrated from Rishikesh and settled down in Delhi. There i wanted to make use of my knowledge to earn but somehow i did not click. The very first case ended me in jail for three months and my family members had to flee to my native place. My wife was dead against me in changing the profession and asked me not to go after money in crooked ways. But did not listen to her and i was happy that she left me on her own with the children. After wards i roamed about the country from state to state and finally found Karnataka where i found the religious leaders were given due respect by the people and the politicians as well .

I waited for an opportunity to settle down. It came in the town of Dharwar. I rented a small one room house – among thick growth of vegetation. I was sitting hours on end meditating right under the glare of the passersby. It lasted for six months when slowly i was approached by a lady having problem with cruel in-laws and husband. I clinched the case and within a month the lady came back to say that her problems had gone and she was happy. Word of mouth brought further cases and within the next year, i had clients from other towns also. Thus i posed as a holy man doing meditation for hours and helped people who needed my services in-between. Thus i acquired the status of a spiritual leader but basically i am witchcraft specialist and a hypnotist only, whether you believe it or not"

Swamiji handed over the mike to the old man and without turning back started getting down from the platform and within a few minutes left the big hall – keeping the audience shocked and mentally shattered.

The VVIPs , VIPs and others did not know what to do next. But the group of holy knew what they should do- they quickly marched out of the hall like the host swamiji. What followed thereafter was shown in TVs . The VVIPs and the other elites silently left the hall bowing down their heads avoiding the flash of the press cameras. The frustration of the devotees knew no bounds but they were disgusted with their own folly in going after holy persons like the swamiji swarga ananda. But they could not believe their ears and eyes though they were confident that they heard and saw the god man openly confessing that he was a cheat.

Then their attention took a turn on the old man but for whom the holy person would have continued for years cheating them posing as a divine personality. Already the media people surrounded the old man and were pestering him to the extent of physically harassing. But the old man telling repeatedly telling the same thing again and again.

13

" I am devotee of the Swargananda and i came to see him in person. I had no idea of asking any question. I was watching the program when suddenly i felt that i should go to the altar and ask the questions. I have never stood up in any stage till now and i am mortally afraid of speaking to a crowd leave alone a gathering of this size. I mechanically followed what prompted me to do. Fortunately my guru called me to come to the altar. I took it as an opportunity to see him at close quarters but when i went there, i talked something without my control. I am not responsible for what had transpired today and i myself feel shocked when the swamijis replied to my question one by one."

But no one believed him but hailed him as eye opener of the society infested with cheats masquerading as spiritual gurus. But that incident was viewed along with the two previous ones when those who were responsible for the miraculous actions reportedly denied having anything to do with what they had done. They also told that some unknown force only forced them and they did not deserve the praise and fame wrongly attributed to their extraordinary power.

The media left with no choice to make a public announcement" who is behind all these incidents ?"

****

INCIDENT- 4

Krishnan was working for a TV company which was started only a year back and it was owned by a political party leader with no scruples and ethics. He was a thug and criminal committing crimes for money. He was spotted by a political leader who used him to subdue all his enemies one by one and in the process, the thug himself was given training in political games. Within five years he became a politician by his own right who was sought after by the leading political parties to make use of his power for political gains.

He liked to be behind the scene and get things done by his stooges. He brought his family members into politics and slowly one by one his son, son-in-law and even his daughter got political positions either as MLA or as MP. At this juncture he wanted to have a TV for projecting his political interests and highlighting his personal glory through telecasts continuously. He had an eye for the chief minister chair and towards achieving his goal he was moving his coins and his family members and supporters worked overtime to boost the image for the party .

In the TV company of this political big wig, Krishnan with his degree in visual communication and a few years apprentice training in big TV companies joined as a full time TV camera man. He was a normal person – minding his own business and not interested in politics. His main interest was to direct a movie at least in the future and he should take up the camera work himself. He resided in the outskirts of Chennai city with his sister's family but his parents were in the village near Theni.

That days program included as usual something connected with the political leader's party or family. The programme executive in charge of

14

organising live programs told Krishnan that they would be interviewing the political boss on that day and he would be questioning him and the live shooting of the interview would be handled by Krishnan. It was ok for Krishnan who had met the boss many times within this six months in some program or other. But what perplexed Krishnan was the additional information given by the team head. The interview would be telecast not only by the TV owned by the boss but other leading TV companies having national and local footing. The reason given by the programme executive was amusing to hear- " our boss wants to become known across the states to enter national politics later after he finishes his stint at the state as CM"

The appointment was fixed at 4.30 pm on a Saturday evening with a dinner slated after the shooting for all the crew members of the medias- which included costliest foreign liquors and valuable gifts to the media men.

Two hours prior to the appointment, Krishnan and his crew were asked to be ready and slowly one by one outboard telecast units of the big TV companies appeared there and started establishing their units on the vast open space surrounding the political boss's farm house. Krishnan felt that at least ten crores of rupees should have been spent for organising such a lavish program, but he did not share it with anyone.

The boss appeared in a simple dhoti plus white full shirt with a towel on his shoulders, wearing the white vibhuthi Prasad with a round kunkum mark in the centre. He had no jewels on him and that was a notable change from his usual public appearances till then- or otherwise he was a walking jewellery shop as per the press reports.

The vantage points were taken over by the big TVs and with the available space, Krishnan was doing his level best to shoot the program. The programme executive who was to ask the questions was at the last minute dropped and in his place a famous TV comperer, a lady, was brought to question the boss.

The questions were so carefully prepared and the boss was so carefully tutored to answer. One by one slowly the boss answered for every question and all over the nation millions of viewers should have watched according to the organisers of the program who took a fat sum from the boss giving a rosy picture about the outcome of the interview which according to them would create a powerful impact in the minds of the people across the nation.

When there were only a few questions left for the lady to ask, suddenly Krishnan gave the video camera to his assistant and jumped before the boss and asked him whether he could ask a question. The TV crew of all the companies were shocked- programme executive was shocked and the viewers of the political party of the boss were also surprised.

The boss looked at Krishnan whom he had seen before with the camera but he had no idea whether it was a part of the program of the day or not. But the live telecast was on and hence he smiled at Krishnan and asked him to go ahead.

The organisers thought that the boss had introduced an element of surprise by allowing his staff to question him instead of the lady. There were lot of confusions when the boss asked Krishnan to ask the question.

Krishnan hesitated for a few seconds only when he asked " Sir, can you tell about your political background and how you have climbed upto this level of political importance?"

The organisers heaved a sigh of relief as the questions were simple which could be easily answered by the political boss without difficulty- of course – it would be a bundle of lies –about sacrifices and unselfish public service and other bullshits .

With his trade mark smile- right under the direct home service telecasting- the boss said quietly and firmly-

" you wanted my political history or my life history – you did not ask me clearly. Any way i would tell everything not only for you but for the whole nation" he stopped and cleared his throat as if he was going to deliver a big speech which he did.

" i was born in a poor family in a village Tamilnadu and Karnataka border. I had no formal education nor regular food. We were three sisters and two brothers My elder brother died when he was twelve years old. All my sisters remained coolies in the farms nearby and two of them married and third one committed suicide because she became pregnant before marriage. My parents died when i was twenty and my sisters threw me out as i was becoming a local rowdy in the village and on and off was arrested and sentenced to jail.

Without any income and relationships, i shifted my activities to Salem and there i picked a few like me and slowly created gang . We did small thefts here and there and gradually established our name in the underground activities by undertaking serious major crimes. I eliminated some of my own gang members for their anti-gang activities and within three years, i became number dada or thug in the district. Murder, rape and other crimes became our daily routine and if we were caught, we managed to get bail as well as silencing the witnesses. We looked after the local police well and in short, i was almost ruling the underground activities unchallenged for two years when the minister of the ruling party sent word for me and made me his body guard and right hand for all his clandestine activities. I had committed many crimes including murder at the request of the minister who gained immense power and he was easily sought after by all the political parties who were voted to rule the state. The minster also switched party affiliation just like changing his dhoti and underwear. He did everything only on one thing- totally relaying on me and my thug-power.

One day he told me that i should become a politician like him and he would make me a MLA and he did it at the next available opportunity. I won three elections as MLA of course using intimidations, bogus votes, muscle power , capturing the booths, and using unlawful and illegal methods to win the elections. In fact, i had to eliminate my own mentor the Minister when he threatened to expose me.

16

My political life is full of irregularities and crimes as otherwise how can rogues like me could become ministers MLA?

Another thing i want to tell now. During the past twenty years of my involvement in active politics i have amassed rupees two hundred thirty nine cores- particularly during the last five years as minister of public works . The money is safely kept in five places – one in a tailed house near my own house in my native place, another one in a house in the busy area of Cochin, the third one in Bangalore and the four one in a school run by family and the last one in Delhi guest house. Besides i have ten kilograms of gold, diamonds, lands, theatres , wine shops, bungalows in Ooty, Goa panaji, Mumbai and of course Chennai.

All put together i may have wealth exceeding five hundred crores, but i donot pay any taxes for the wealth and income from my pocket. They are paid by people who come to seek favour for them.

When such is my background history, do you know what are my ambitions in life? I want to become the chief minister after the next election and after two terms i would like to make my son as the CM and i want to move on to the centre to start with to become a minister and to end up with the post of the Prime Minister before i retire from active politics.

Whether i have qualifications to become a CM or a PM, i have the power of money, backed up by the rowdies who would do what i say including murders besides, the support of the unscrupulous business persons, corrupt police and government officers- to top it all- my party cadres who are low class ruffians and thugs. Who can stop me from achieving my ambitions?"

The boss laughed for a few minutes and his story of self confession became an instant hit in the world news. He was blissfully not aware of the impact of his own admissions to the crimes including the murder of the minister who was his mentor.

The political party to which he belonged as a Minister, the people who happened to view the program across the nation through the famous TV channels were flabbergasted by the open admission of crimes by a minister of the ruling party of Tamilnadu.

The main opposition party at the state and the centre had already started voicing their demand for arresting the minister and confiscate the enormous wealth accumulated through illegal means. Krishnan escaped miraculously and fled from Chennai. He was reported to be staying with his distant cousin in Kanpur.

But the whole world, the Media people, the public across the states were all praise for Krishnan and in fact, there was habeas corpus petition before High court of Tamil nadu to produce Krishnan before the court. The petitioners claimed that the minister and his gangs would have harmed Krishnan and as such the demand for the searching for Krishnan was gaining momentum from day by day.

But the poor Krishnan was telling his cousin " Vitchu(Viswanathan short form) I was shooting the program when suddenly i felt that i should go to my boss and ask permission to question him. Even at that time i did not know what questions i wanted to ask. But i was shocked when i was permitted by my boss to go ahead and ask. It was further shocking when my boss started accepting all his crimes and how he did it and how he made money and how he came to be a minister and finally the amount of wealth he made misusing his position. Vitchu- i cannot make anyone to tell the truths and how my questions made the criminal boss to own all his crimes- i still cannot digest. But one thing, i cannot go back to Chennai or see my sister or go to native place to see my parents" he was crying.

As usual his cousin did not believe what his cousin told him but treated him with respect and fear for the extraordinary powers he possessed.

INCIDENT- 5

The Nehru auditorium was full to the last seat. All tickets were sold out. Even the extra seating arrangement to accommodate the recommended categories of last minute guests was full.

The occasion was the seventy fifth anniversary of Indian cinema industry in India. It was first of the four grand events programmed all over the country to mark the platinum jubilee of cinema which had made inroads in every field of activities of Indians. The Tamil nadu film federation jointly with the all India body took up the organisational work, program sponsored by business and industries giants and the invitations were made to all the leading actors of all languages for all the four events- one at Chennai, the second one at Kolkata, the third one at Delhi and the grand finale at Mumbai.

Special traffic arrangements shook the city normal traffic and the tickets were priced very high as the highlights of the programs consisted of several firsts in the industries long history of mega events. It was a program when south Indian fans could see all the top actors not only of Indian movies but also of the great Hollywood matinee idols. The event would inaugurated by the Prime Minister at Chennai and the closing ceremony would be taken up by the President of India.

Around one hundred thousand cheerful looking fans of assorted age from all the four south based states were present in the ten storied gallery. At the ground level- the vast area was accommodating the VIP actors in the front three rows and behind them the producers, technical persons, and others directly and indirectly connected with the film industry over the past seventy five years were seated. Whenever their favourite actors entered the hall of the events, they stood up to shout slogans of long life for the actors. The warm welcome cry of the fans repeated several times till the Prime Minister along with the state governor arrived. As a mark of respect to the Prime Minster all those who were present stood up till the chief guest took his chair in the centre of the row of dignitaries which included the state Chief minister, the president of all Indian film chamber, Senior actors of yesteryears of the four zones of the country, President of Nadigar sangam (actors guild) and other VIPs like central minister for information and public entertainment . The program was compeered by the Karnataka heart throb – an actress well known in four languages including Tamil and Hindi. The program started with the prayer to goddess for Tamil language. Then followed the welcome address by the President of the All India Film Federation –a famous film producer in Hindi owning studios in India and abroad. He welcomed the Prime Minster and other dignitaries while briefly giving the history of film industry in India. He was followed up by the President of Tamil nadu film federation who spoke about the Tamil film industry in detail. At the end of his speech the irritated fans felt happy by whistling repeatedly to mark the end of a boring lecture.

Then the doyen of Indian film industry and the old but still young hero of hundreds of Hindi movies Naresh Kumar took the mike and the whole crowd went up in hysterics to see their favourite actor in flesh and blood before them.

The actor majestically waved at the crowds of fans and sent flying kisses to show his affection and love for them. He then spoke-

" i am indeed honoured to be the first speaker on this great occasion to mark the beginning of the seventy fifth year of the entertainment industry in the country. But"....before he could continue- one of the compeerers – the sweet little actress from Kannada films- intervened and asked whether she could ask him a question.

The thousands of fans present stood up and booed out to show their displeasure over the interruption of the speech by their hero. But the hero himself though was confused over the sudden intervention from an unexpected quarters, yet managed to wear a smile and like a great hero of films, bowed before the cute girl and asked her to proceed.

The girl thanked the great film star and looked at the dais and the row of VVIPs. With an excuse she blurted out-

"sir, you have been an actor for fifty years and more. You have made millions of rupees by acting. Can you tell this august audience that you have paid all your genuine taxes to the government in return for the opportunities to make money given to you till now?"

The program was not fortunately telecasted live and hence other than those who were lucky enough to be present at the stadium could not have heard or seen what the girl asked the great actor. But the VVIPs were becoming restless, the organisers were losing their emotional control, the police personnel were waiting for the signal to throw the girl out and the crowd shouted in filthy language asking the girl to get lost or else face the consequences.

The actor stood frozen but the girl stared at him.

The whole thing lasted for 120 seconds or less. Before the police women constables could rush to the stage and pull the girl out, the actor beefed up a sheepish smile and addressed the crowd-

" please please be calm – don't shout- she has not abused me or said filthy words about me or the persons present. She only asked me whether i have paid my dues to the government. She was right in asking because, i

19

earned from your income through the movies and i should do my duty of contributing to the government which is extending all types of services to you – is it not? Please sit down and i will answer the question. I request the police not to get panicky and others interested in me to let the girl free"

He then walked a few steps towards the row of VVIPs and veered back to face the public and said-

" my dear young girl- you are right- i have not paid my dues – though i have paid something- but the major part of what i have earned remained without being shown as my real income till now. I have earned a lot and spent a lot. I have accounts in foreign banks- have flats in foreign cities- assets i have in USA and Switzerland- but i have not disclosed anything to any government authorities till now. May be in the eyes of the government i am an offender of law- may be i have to pay around two hundred seventy crores as taxes to the government till; now. That was only my own rough estimate which i made a few years back while sitting alone in my Kulu valley guest house, looking at the snow fall. The amount is staggeringly high because of the steep income tax for higher incomes in the country. Anyway i have not paid and it is a fact. I do not include my son and my daughter in law besides my wife. May be all of us put together we may have to pay to government of India around five hundred crores today."

He paused for a few seconds and looked at the girl straight and asked her – " you wanted this information is it not? Now you have got it. Tell me what else you want to know"

The girl looked down and when she raised her hear she was shedding tears profusely.

"Sir, i asked the question not to snub you or make you a criminal in the presence of all those who are present. But i request you to call Vijay Mehta the super star of Hindi film today to come to the stage and answer the same question". The crowd that time kept quiet and the dignitaries did not know what was happening there.

Naresh Kumar looked at the present day super star and asked him to come to the stage. There was dead silence in that big auditorium and everybody looked at the direction of the super star who was nuzzling in his seat. He was again called upon to come to the stage when he stood up shakily and looking back at the crowd of fans and other actors like him- went up the stage and shook hands with the senior super star. They embraced for a few seconds and then Naresh Kumar handed over the mike to him and asked him to reply to the question of the girl.

But the girl intervened and said- " sir, you are the super hero today and you have several hits recently over the past five years. Were you responsible for any incident that might have cost the life of others till now?"

Everyone present was surprised- they expected to hear from the super star about his tax evasions. But the girl asked him a different question altogether.

Vijay Mehta struggled to speak for a few minutes. But the girl was staring at him as she did at Naresh kumar.

Finally he managed to hold the mike properly and spoke-not looking at any one in present but at the ceiling of the auditorium-

" yes – you are right girl- i was responsible for the loss of life of one person" he paused for a few seconds. The crowd looked aghast with the admission of the guilty by their super hero. They were anxiously waiting for what he going to tell further when the hero continued-

" yes- i have only pushed my wife from behind from the balcony of my three storied building. She crashed down and died instantly. But i quietly left the balcony and went to my room and took a strong doze of liquor and started to forget what i had done. I wanted someone from the family or servants to find the body and i should get the news of the accident from others. It happened as i had planned. I was woken up from my fake sleep and my young daughter told me the bad news while crying for her mother. Me and my actress wife had disagreement over many things but we kept our conflicts brawls and verbal altercations and attacks within our spacious bedroom and outside we had decided not to hurt the feelings of our children. It helped me to act in real life and my criminal act was accepted as a natural accident and i .." he stopped and could not continue as he was choking with emotions.

But somehow he managed to talk further-" girl you have made to tell the truth and here i am standing before all of you as a criminal who instead of settling the matter in a divorce court committed a grave   mistake – because- she tortured me with her words and verbal attacks about many personal things. At one time i was planning to go for legal separation for which she did not agree. She wanted me to suffer and suffer till my end and she would not give me freedom to spoil another woman- she vowed. I am sorry but whether sorry for the crime is acceptable to law i do not know. Further i want to do what my senior did- i also hid my income and many investments in India and abroad. Between me and my senior here, i had produced a few films on my own budget and squandered crores of rupees. I have earned and have lost also. But still i have to pay the taxes to the government. The recent hits if added to the my wealth would come anywhere near three hundred crores within a ten year span of film acting- and i might have paid only a fraction of it as tax. Hence on that count also i stand before you all –" he looked at the Prime Minister who was looking spell bound by the revelations of the top cine actors one by one.-" as a criminal of concealing income and defaulter of tax dues in crores.

My dear girl- you, i have replied to your question which you directly asked and also for the question which you have asked through my senior artist. Jai Hind" the hero stylishly handed down the mike to the stunned girl and marched towards his seat with his head bent down in shame.

There was not even a whisper anywhere the audience.

No one knew what to do next. The row of dignitaries looked aghast with shock- the actors and others present looked frozen and the crowd remain transfixed. But the girl called for the super star of the Tamil movie –Surya Kant to come to the stage.

The super star normally looking boisterous with overflowing enthusiasm not matching his age- was not responding to the call. He looked as if he had not heard anything. But when the girl called him to come again he had to get up- because- he did not know what to do at that point of time when the whole crowd of fans was waiting for him to come out like the other two greats in the film world.

Slowly he stood up and without looking anywhere- he ran up to the stage in his usual style and took the mike from the girl and started immediately-

" I know what the girl is going to ask me- hence, let me reply to the question she has not asked"

The girl wanted to tell something but the hero continued –" just like my colleagues in the film industry, i have also defaulted in paying the tax dues on my genuine income. It may be in crores – but one thing which i would like to tell everyone present- i am ready to pay all the dues to the government provided the money which i give should be used for the welfare of the people and not for the personal enrichment of the politicians. Is there any government in the country which can assure me that not only my tax dues but the dues of all my colleagues present here would be used only for the public welfare? Come on- i want an assurance " so saying he looked at the Prime Minister who was avoiding his direct visual attack on him and also the camera focus on him.

" my dear fans – all the actors earn from your income only as said by Nareshji. But like you we are also watching the performance of the governments at the state and the central levels- so many mega-frauds- scandals- corruption in thousands of crores- misuse of public welfare projects for personal enrichment- whether it is fodder for animals or cremation grounds for the dead- sports events, communication licences- you name any activity – we find the cruel hands of corrupt officials and political leaders. Under these circumstances, if we do not pay the taxes and spend them directly for the benefit of the people would it not be better? I thought during one of my trips to a holy place. I decided that i should do something to return the portion of my income to the fans who are first in the list of beneficiaries – it was their income which i was guaranteed to get and next came the general public. Till taking the noble decision, i did not pay the taxes due on my genuine income and after taking the conscious decision seven years back- i am honestly telling you that i have repaid a portion of my income to my fans and general public without making any publicity. Even my wife is not aware of it – only my legal advisor and political critic knew what i was doing besides the beneficiaries who got the financial help in some form or other through my trusted friends who have promised to keep the matter as a top secret and i am happy to add that till now they have not violated their promises.

Now my dear girl- i have told what you expected me to tell and also more than what you did not expect. The amount of my income received so far- the amount of expenditure i have incurred for the welfare measures completed till now-the amount of taxes i have paid and finally the amount of the taxes i have to pay as per the Income tax rules would be worked out within a month and i promise you and others present that i would place everything before the competent authorities and await their reactions like a good taxpaying salary earning- middle class citizen. Right" He hugged the girl for a few seconds and as usual ran down the few steps to his seat.

The crowd hitherto remaining dumbfounded sprang up from their seats and shouted at their top of their voice- " Long live Surya- the super star of all times- you are great " many such encomiums were heard from all sides of the stadium and even the dignitaries clapped their hands unconsciously.

What next followed was most unexpected- one after another – all the film producers- actors hurriedly left the hall without turning this side or that side. They also ran away from the possible call from the girl. After fifteen minutes of that exodus- only the crowd remained baffled by the sudden turn of events- the three actors who replied to the questions did not move away from the seats .

The Prime minister got up followed by the governor and the CM- they all left the stage without uttering one word to any one of the organisers and eventually the event came to an end abruptly.

But the girl remained alone with the mike.

The police sprang up with actions. Two women constables rushed to the stage and took the girl outside while the president of Nadikar sangam took the mike and announced with profuse apologies that the program could not be continued for the reasons known to them. But the crowd was not in the mood to listen but reacted very badly by throwing the chairs, throwing whatever came to their hands, shouting in filthy languages demanding the ticket money back immediately. They started damaging the furniture and the electrical fittings and moved dangerously towards the TV crew and the remaining members of the organising committee. The police expecting some such untoward incidents, already called for additional strength of the riot police who rushed in wielding bamboo shields and shouting at the mob to clear away from the hall.

Within a few minutes the hall bore the brunt of a war like situation when the crowds with uncontrolled emotions threw the water bottles, empty cans, even threw the chairs after uprooting them from the base. It took one hour for the police team to chase away the crowd and close the auditorium which looked as if an earthquake took place exclusively inside the hall.

Media coverage continued amidst warlike situation and the entire nation was stunned by the happenings at the inaugural function of the film platinum jubilee.

The police took the girl compereer to the commissioner office and there she was interrogated to find out her motives and her power to extract truth from people.

She was repeating only what those who were responsible for similar earlier episodes like the court case of the ex-minister, the accident spot at Sholinganallur –the religious function where the holy men confessed on their own.

" madam(to the women police officer) i tell you i do not know what had happened there at the stage. I went there to compeer but the minute the actor started talking, i felt that i should intervene and ask some questions. I did not what were the questions at that time. But i asked. Why and how- i do not know please"

The top police authorities had a high power meeting and discussed the similarities of the four cases reported till then. Except the case of the Minister who confessed to the crimes when questioned by the TV camera man, in all the other cases the persons who questioned told gave the same reason that some force had egged them to ask the questions and left to them they were not capable of extracting truth from any one. The police top brasses came to the conclusion that there was something else to the case which did not meet the eye. Someone with super power was behind the four cases and that someone picked up innocent persons to act on that person's behalf. But the fact remained that because of the unknown force, many truths were brought to lime light- like the murder of the wife of the Hindi super star- the murder of a minister of Tamil nadu government, the black money and the amount of tax evasion by the cine actors.

The Direct general of Police wound up the meeting with a warning to the top officials that the unknown person or power was not an enemy of the state. No action should be taken without consulting him and the government by any police personnel. He felt that the super power person could do what he or she wanted openly and legally instead of using the innocent people to remove the social ills. But he himself continued that if that super person came out openly, he would not be allowed to do what he or she wanted and might be openly killed .

His final remarks before the end of the meeting was –" let us wait and watch"

INCIDENT-6

On the next day morning, the Kilpauk Chennai police station sprang into action upon receiving an urgent call from the city's top educationist residence. The station was headed by an Asst commissioner. When the call was received the station House officer Sarathy rang up the inspector-crime branch and gave the information received over phone who in turn - did the same thing to the AC forthwith.

By the time the police team arrived at the posh eight grounds mansion like residence of the Chancellor of Swaroop Deemed University Dr.Ponal mangalam there were hundreds of visitors who got the news before the police besides the usual press fellows with flash lights ready cameras, running here and there questioning everyone to find out what they knew about the previous night's tragedies that struck the family members of the chancellor.

When the inspector Mariappan a senior inspector waiting for promotion within a month arrived with his men, the scenario changed. The people gathered there were requested to leave the premises and the press people were asked to wait. The inspector went through the biggest house-entrance ever seen by ordinary people- the Burmese teak carved doors were fit for exhibition and the black granite walls on both the sides added a majestic beauty only tons of money could get.

In the palatial hall where the close relatives and the top officials of the colleges and University were present with fear written all over their faces. The five grand children of the chancellor were crying hugged by their relatives consoling them frequently.

The Vice chancellor Dr.Arulanandam the next in command of the educational institutions of Dr. Ponal Mangalam, greeted the inspector and without waiting for the formal question from the inspector told him-

" sir, around three in the morning i received a call from the chancellor's residence from the servants who reported a gruesome scene at the house. They were crying and terribly agitated. I told them to wait and look after the family members while contacting the hospitals to rush their ambulances to take the victims for immediate treatment. I then informed the police control room and all the senior colleagues and rushed to this place to take charge of everything till you people arrive. I reside at the University campus and it took twenty minutes to reach here. I have seen to that –nothing is touched and no one entered the rooms or other areas for you to do your job without difficulty."

He himself was run down with tension. He was profusely perspiring and needed treatment himself.

" Half an hour back the ambulances have come and have taken all the twelve victims to the hospital along with senior officers and here I am looking after the children, the VIPs who are coming here upon getting the information managing the press to the extent possible" he was wiping his eyes to ward off the tear drops from the sight of the police officer.

The inspector looked around and by then the official photographers arrived at the scene of crime and the police dogs were on the way along with the fingerprint and forensic experts.

"Sir you have been telling that the twelve victims were seriously injured. But the information i have at the police station was vague . Can you tell me what you have seen when you arrived here and what were the injuries you have noticed on the twelve persons?- the inspector was asking plainly

The VC hesitated for a few seconds and upon clearing the throat said- " inspector- what can i tell you or how can i tell you- " he was actually crying uncontrollably- Ponal Mangalam treated him as his closest friend for the past fifteen years when he was identified and offered a top position at the college of the Ponal Mangalam

"sir, the eyes and ears were totally burnt – in the case of my friend Ponal and his first son-and for others, the injuries were different –Mrs Ponal was burnt to the extent of a big hole on both her hands- the second son and the two sons-in-laws received serious injuries to both his thighs- the criminal had not spared the ladies also. Their faces were smeared with acid deeply – i could see burnt bones on their faces. What he did to burn the eyes and other parts of the body- i did not know. But the acrid smell of highly concentrated sulphuric acid attacked my nose when i entered this hall where the victims were wriggling with pain with half consciousness. That meant – the victims had a strong dose of anaesthesia or chloroform or some such thing to make them lose consciousness when he did the gruesome act of burning the eyes ears, hands and thighs. That bastard- if only i get hold of him, i would not mind being hanged i would kill him with my bare hands" the VC became hysteric and needed badly some rest and tranquilizers.

The inspector called one of the police personnel and told him to take care of the VC and take him to nearby clinic for rest and treatment . But the VC refused but the inspector was firm but kind.

The police cordoned off the residence of the chancellor, declared holidays of all the educational institutions run by the same family- ransacked the surroundings, interrogated the security personnel threadbare- actually they were looking threadbare after the police treatment- fifteen teams searching for any clue which would take them to the criminal. The media was pestering the commissioner of police and the DGP seeking the latest development in tracing the culprit.

Despite the most torturous treatment given to the five security persons who were on guard on that unfortunate night, they were repeating the same thing-

" sir, we were doing our duty till ten in the night- three of us at the front gate including the two of us roaming around the bungalow continuously. This is in addition to the kitchen staff and servants remaining awake on that night till midnight without whose notice nothing could happen . They are staying with their families at the servants quarters – four families and two bachelors – a driver and general assistant – all were personally recruited by the chancellor and his wife only. Sir, after ten thirty what happened we did not know. When we woke up around three we could not see or speak immediately. We felt vomiting and dizzy. Some nasty foul smell came from our security room. This is the truth sir, they were begging with folded hands and crying.

The Director General of police and the commissioner discussed the matter one to one and in the end – they felt why that gruesome injury could not have been inflicted by the super force- they shuddered to think about such a possibility. It was because the history of the so called educationist was full of pending cases for murder, rape, thefts, ransoms, political crimes. He started his life as a peon in the post office in the city. He then took the avatar of an auto driver – a pimp- a rowdy and finally a gang leader when he was taken as trusted lieutenant of a political leader. During that time when he was sure of his political patronage and the indirect freedom from police he was a terror in the city . But he was not appearing before the public nor he was troubling the people. He was after people with money and power. Thus he had accumulated 129 cases where the police could do nothing but to call him for so called interrogation and with the false readymade alibis, the police found it convenient to let him off as he was having the blessings from the ruling party while the FIRs filed were kept as old records in the police department , probably waiting for the completion of the prescribed period for destruction. But how such a criminal became the top educationist in the country was the secret doubt of all the true to the profession police officers till the last few years, when the government itself honoured him with a state honour and the central government decorated him with the highest award for his noble services in the field of education.

The two top police officials of the state after going through the past criminal records of Ponal Mangalam found out the reason for the meteoric raise of the ex-post office peon- from the underworld stage to the present stage of international recognition- one- the hundreds of thugs or killers he was keeping under his pay roll for several years till now ready to execute the orders of their boss whether it was murder or kidnap and murder and two- the unquestionable political support from all the leading parties who were looked after beyond their satisfaction in every possible way .

There were press people or knowledgeable persons in the state who knew the name and fame for the ex-post office peon were all bought with the filthy money obtained as capitation fees received from the students all over the country for the past fifteen years.

After three days of top class treatment by the local, national and international doctors, the result was tragic and disappointing. Two of the twelve members of the chancellor family lost both eye sights and hearing permanently and the others lost the use of the burnt hands and legs completely. The ladies face looked so gruesome- the panel of doctors had decided to call for plastic surgery specialists from abroad though they were doubtful whether it would restore the normal appearance. What the doctors did was to stop further damage in all cases. But there also they could not help the chancellor and his eldest son- apart from the eyes and ears, in their cases- certain core functions of the body were also affected-resulting in total malfunction of some of the organs of control. They would remain as cripples till their end.

The police department was waiting for the chancellor to become fit enough to tell what really happened on that fateful night.

That he did on the fourth day early morning when he woke up suddenly and asked for the top police to come as he wanted to tell them something.

Commissioner with a battalion of police officers rushed to the five star specialty hospital as the Director general of police was away to his native place to attend a funeral of his close relative. He was of course informed duly.

When the commissioner Bal Krishna Nair entered the spacious room fully packed with latest medical equipment, a relative who was present with the chancellor shook him. She wrote something on his hand with her fingers to tell him that the police officer had come . Getting up from the bed with difficulty and groping in the air with his hands widely swinging here and there, the chancellor almost cried –" sir, you have come – please come here as i cannot see or hear you. But that does not matter- you can hear " the words were flowing non-stop as the chancellor would not be able to hear what he was telling but only could feel through the words coming out of his mouth.

The commissioner had seen him on many occasions before and had been the guest of the educationist during the college and university functions. But on that day he was moved to tears to see that powerful and strong person even at the age of seventy plus- behaving erratically while talking aimlessly.

He patted him on his hand and wrote on his hand like his relative that the police would do everything to punish the guilty as early as possible.

" commissioner sir, you want to know what had happened on that night. I will tell you. After dinner we –that is- me and my why used to go for a walk around our bungalow and sit at the lawn for a few minutes before retiring to our first floor bed room. Now- a-days my two sons and my sons in law look after my business, educational institutions and i am almost retired except giving directions on important issues.

That night after ten thirty little early for us to go to our bed room. But I normally pray in the Christ room- named by my grandson, before going to bed room while others would do it at the bed room itself. When i just returned after the usual prayer, i saw someone standing in the middle of the hall- the hall lights were switched off except the two central lights of low voltage by the servants. I could not see the person clearly. Hence when i started moving towards the person asking him who he was and what he wanted. But that was the last thing i remember clearly now. Thereafter, for the past three days, i was breaking my head to find out what i did after going towards the person- i could not recollect. But vaguely something comes to my mind on and off—i was dropping something in the eyes and ears of my son, the same thing on the palms- on the thighs- on the face of others- i do not remember on whom exactly Sometimes i get another thing in my mind- i was asking my sons, daughter in laws and wife and others to come to my room immediately "

He was holding his head and shaking violently and crying aloud, " Oh Jesus – please do not torture me – do not punish me like this- Jesus save me – "

On seeing the pathetic conditions of the old man- the attending doctor administered some medicine through injection and within a few minutes blabbering something the great educationist plunged into silence- might be deep sleep or unconsciousness only the doctor knew

The commissioner after patting the unfortunate victim, wanted to meet the others in the hospital one by one to know whether they were willing to tell something that might give a lead to the arrest of the culprit still at large.

The wife of Ponal Mangalam was appearing to be a pious old lady. Unless her husband she was quite and calm. On seeing him entering her room,

28

she greeted him. The police chief wanted to say some formal words of comfort to console her.

But the lady said in her matter of fact tone- ' Sir whatever you do now, i have lost my hands. Can i get them back?" there was a trace of sadness in her words.

When the COP wanted to know what had happened on that night- she simply said –" my husband came to our bedroom and asked me to come down. I accompanied him to the hall through the stair case,. That was the last thing i knew. Thereafter i woke up with pain all over the my right hand where i saw vaguely a big hole with blood oozing from gaping wound. . I remember to have been brought to the hospital and thereafter i woke up only two days before. Within the two days i heard what no one should hear. Some enemy of our family took the sight and hearing power of my husband and my first son, destroyed the faces of my daughters, my daughter in laws and the legs of my second son and my two sons- in law. Why? What was that person going to gain by depriving us of these the vital organs? Why he did not choose to kill us instead-that would have been better for us." After a few minutes she continued amidst shedding tears- " that person wanted not to kill us but to make us die every day without able to see or hear – or walk or pick up something in this world till we die naturally"

The same case like her husband- she went into uncontrollable spasm and the doctor instantly gave her a stab of some morphine or sleeping dose- she stopped talking and crying slowly and finally went into deep sleep.

But the commissioner could leave the rest of the affected persons without making the preliminary enquiry now that they were medically fit for interview if not interrogation of police style.

Hence the police chief persisted in his efforts to get some semblance of clue to solve the case but all the rest of ten victims repeated almost like the wife of the chancellor- that they were asked to come down to hall by their father over the phone and they remember to have come down but that was the last thing they remembered about the incident.

The commissioner scratched his head and left the hospital with his deputies who also were as confused as their boss. That was not the day for the police- the commissioner told himself while going to his office .

At the police head quarters, meetings after meetings were held but there was no significant progress in the case of acid victims of the educationist and his family. Director General of police and the commissioner both were fired by the Chief Minister who demanded results as early as possible as he was not able to meet the press and the opposition parties at the assembly The two top guns of police could only promise and report the deployment of thousand expert police investigators immediately by them in twenty five teams. But the CM was not satisfied with their explanations.

But the chiefs of police felt that the attack on the family of the educationist could be the handy work of the unknown power only.

Their guess was right. Two days after the return of the DGP from his personal visit, to the HQ, a courier mail cover heavily secured with lot of tapes and warnings that the contents were meant for only the DGP. The PRO office which received the parcel looked at it with the usual police suspicion and subjected the courier mail to scanning and bomb squad checking. The contents were declared to be free from any explosive material and it was safe to open. But the sender had clearly warned that it should be opened only the DGP or commissioner. Hence, the police PRO took the cover to the DGP office at the first floor left hand side corner and handed over the same to the PA of the top official. He also told him that the parcel had been checked thoroughly to confirm that it could be opened safely by the addressee- namely the DGP.

After half- on-hour when the meeting on some urgent official matters was over, the PA took the parcel and handed it over to chief. He looked at the parcel from various angles and saw the efforts taken by the sender to see that the parcel was opened only by the addressee, by the multiple cello-tapes over the edges and all sides with the word 'warning' written with the sketch pen. He hesitated for a few seconds and asked the PA to open it – despite the bomb squad certificate attached with the parcel.

Inside the thick cover, there was one more plastic cover and inside – there was a Disc and a bunch of hand written A4 size papers. When the DGP quickly went through the contents, he stood up and was almost shouting ' Oh God" and was holding the papers in his left hand was shaking his head to show his disbelief and shock.

He then ordered his PA to contact the COP (commissioner) to come to DGP office immediately and also other senior officials to report to him forthwith.

He sat down and went through the five pages hand written letter or rather a confession by the educationist Dr Ponal Mangalam carefully and when he had completed the reading all the pages, he quickly looked inside the parcel and took out a disc which he inserted in his computer. There he saw the educationist reading the contents of the letter word by word and finally confirmed that he only wrote the confession letter without being compelled by any one and the police could take possession of all his ill-gotten wealth in form of property documents, cash and other valuables at the places mentioned by him. There was no mention about the acid injuries or about the sighting of a person in the centre of the big drawing hall or about his asking his family members to come down to the ground floor.

The next two hours were so crucial for the police bosses who assembled there in the DGP room at his instruction – they read the contents again and again and finally confirmed the hand of the super power without an iota of doubt . The DGP then rang up the PA of the CM and asked for an urgent appointment with him in connection with the acid burns case. Within a few minutes, the PA conveyed the information that the DGO could meet the CM at 1 PM at his residence. The CM reportedly had cancelled a confirmed program at Tiruchi in the afternoon just to hear the news about the acid burn case.

Around 4 PM the CM gave permission to the DGP to proceed as per rules to arrest the educationist and his son on the grounds of committing heinous crimes of murder, rape and forcibly acquiring properties of others without their consent, deploying thugs and paid criminals to eliminate those who were giving problems to the educationist in the business transactions, personal life and political activities.

In the press meeting the DGP gave the gist of the confessions of the educationist- wherein the details of the crimes he had committed from the beginning of his criminal history and the crimes committed by his on his own including raping of six college girls and silencing their parents with threats of life and money. The confession according to the police chief included the details of the ill-gotten wealth and where the money and the property documents were hidden or kept in benami names- and the list of thugs or killers who were involved in the murder of seven persons and serious physical injury on eleven students and fifty eight business persons and others including the lover of his daughter.

But the press asked the police officer the billion dollar question- whether they could find the criminal who had caused serious injuries to the family members of the educationist. The DGP sheepishly assured the media reporters that the person responsible would be arrested shortly as the police had certain clear clues which might result in cracking the case; actually both the parties of the press meet knew that there was no such clues .

INCIDENT -7

In-between the old and the latest cases of acid attack , the unknown power did not leave the police to take rest .

A murder case pending against a holy man and his ashram-mates came to an end with the holy man openly confessing in the court before the judge that he had to commit the serious offence because he was caught red handed while molesting a woman devotee by the Prohit or Pandit of the temple who came to meet him in connection with the forthcoming festival in his temple. He added that he took the help of his disciples who sought the help of the criminals to eliminate the pandit the witness for the unholy act of a holy man. He finally ended pleading guilty and so saying he took a small box from his hip hidden by the dhoti he was wearing and from there he removed a small tablet like thing and swallowed it while standing in the witness box. He immediately collapsed on the witness box floor itself - dead.

The judge and those who were present at the court- were petrified to see the tragedy of a holy man after admitting the crime which he should not have committed after calling himself religious and spiritual leader for decades. The police arrested others who abetted the crime including the criminals who actually performed the hacking to death of the Pandit in cold blood.

Again the police stood confused as to why a holy man confessed to the crime during a routine hearing of the case which he was denying for the past five years, and also influencing the witnesses one by one to turn hostile against the prosecution to weaken the case gradually which he succeeded till then.

At his residence the commissioner was telling his wife confidentially that the death of the holy man must be due to the unknown force only. But he looked considerably relieved by the closure of the long pending holy man murder case and shared his feelings in a lighter vein with his wife -thus " off late the super power is taking care of law and order of the state –that too- effectively."

INCIDENT-8

Within a few days, in the top official meeting room, the senior officers of Tamil Nadu police along with the head of the district HQs were reviewing the state of affairs prevailing generally and law and order particularly in Tamilnadu. The forensic department head wanted to share an important information about the recent chain of unexpected voluntary confessions. Every one present instantly became alert and anxious to hear what the specialist was going to tell.

" sir, we have extensively analysed every bit of evidence in the four cases of confession and one case of traffic accident and in the process, we took the video clips for micro-examination of the court halls, the venue where the religious function was conducted, the residence of the educationist and the junction of roads where an accident was amicably settled to find out whether there were any points of similarities either in form of the same person appearing in all the cases or any striking sequences of happenings or any unusual happening in the venues of confession prior to or at the time of or after the confession . "

He took a brief second to resume –to conclude-" to our disappointment we could not trace any similarity in the cases so far reported. But hundreds of questions remain unanswered. How and in what form the unknown person came to the scene of confessions, particularly in the case of the residence of the educationist, the court where the holy man committed suicide and in other cases how he picked up the stooges to ask the questions which prompted the criminals to confess to the crimes? But one thing is strikingly clear- some strong tactics with or without the power of mantras or witchcraft should have been exercised to make the victims to forget the face of the person who influenced them to ask questions or the criminals to confess. At the moment it appears to be out of the reach of the modern technology but this cannot continue forever and the culprit is bound to commit some mistake sooner or later" before he could even complete the sentence- there was loud tap on the main door of the meeting room and when it was opened by the senior officer very near to the door,

the PA of the DGP rushed in and went straight to the boss and whispered something in his ears. Upon getting the information, the DGP stood up shocked and blurted out-
"The unknown force had attacked again- this time- the political party leader and his family from Sirkhali town- have been taken into task." He looked at the DIG of the concerned district and asked him to proceed immediately to take charge of the situation and report.

By the time, the local town police inspector and the HQ's SP and other higher officials, including government higher-ups appeared at the scene of attack- one by one- and the situation was getting out of control every minute. There was an urgent message to state HQ to supplement additional force to avert riots and civil commotion –instigated by the party cadres of the burnt leader and his only son in his own residence fully roped to a pillar in the corner of the ground floor hall.

Media got wind of the attack and they managed to be present with their top ranking reporters as the person done in was having a following in most of the districts in deep south of the state.

The SP in charge of the team of police force at the scene of crime-got the first hand information one by one from those who happened to be the direct witness to the gruesome incident . First he called for the securities who were there at the gate of the farm house of the leader at the time of crime.

"sir, we were two at the gate besides there were seven body guards staying inside the compound always taking turn to roam around the campus – stretching out an area of one acre of land – with garden and a small pond but not a swimming pool. In addition to this seven guards, there were servants like cook, car drivers, house maids and gardener staying at the backyards of the farm but outside the border of it. Thus sir, at any time, there were lot of people in the farm and we are at the gate to screen the people before getting permission from the family member to allow them an entry inside." The SP was visibly irritated and demanded what happened on the previous day night only leaving the work profile etc.

The two securities already received the quota of beating from the party local bosses, started blabbering when the SP demanded the details they knew only about the attack on the previous day.

" sir, we were there at the gate keeper room when an auto driver asked us to come out as someone wanted to see us. It was around eleven in the night. He (pointing out to the persons with bruises on his face and hands) only went out to see who wanted to see us. But he came back and asked me to come out with him which i did. That was the last thing we remember sir. " he was crying looking terribly afraid of the police treatment which he heard to extract truth from the witnesses and criminals.

The SP's anger knew no bounds. He simply barked controlling his raging temper as many persons both from the party and from public along with media crew were watching the interrogation by the SP.

" did any of you see who wanted to see you both?"

There was silence for a few seconds but quickly both of them replied that they had seen only the auto man but could not remember whether there was somebody inside the auto or not.

"can you at least identify the auto driver or do you remember the auto number?" the SP thundered.

The two looked blank and said in chorus- "sir, we do not know what happened and do not remember whether we have seen the face of the auto driver or the auto rickshaw number"

The SP looked at them contemptuously and asked his deputy to take them to station for further interrogation .

He then asked the servants one by one who gave the news to the fire station and the police station when the flames started coming out from the windows and the front entrance.

" Sir we have completed the work of the day and as usual retired to our quarters behind the farm house. We saw the guards, on the normal rounds . But there was nothing suspicious We all slept after the tiresome work every day at the bungalow in entertaining hundreds of guests. Only when someone shouted about flames erupting from the windows of the bungalow, did we rush up to see what was about. The front entrance was totally blocked by flames with intense heat. Back entrance was locked inside for safety purpose by us before we left the bungalow from the front entrance. We raised alarm and within a few minutes all the neighbours within a earshot distance came running responding to our cries. All of us started surrounded the bungalow pouring water through the windows and the burning front doors There was no trace of the body guards; on that day -six of the seven were present as we only served them food . When we went to see what the securities were doing without appearing on the scene to help us during the crisis, we found them sleeping. We poured water over them and took them into task . But soon we realised that they were unconscious and actually were not sleeping. "

One of the servants − stopped when another one continued:

" sir, i ran outside the compound gate and asked everyone around the farm house to rush down and help us to stop the fire before it completely destroyed the house and the people inside. The crowd grew in numbers and they all did their best to get water for putting out the fire. At that time, i saw a piece of sari hanging from the door of the car which was parked in the first car shed. There are four covered car parking sheds at the right hand side of the compound. I wanted to check what it was . Sir, inside , i saw" he hesitated − " inside our madam lying unconscious. I was taken aback on seeing the naked body and asked some ladies who were present from the nearby huts to come and clothe the unconscious madam and also to bring out the person for taking to the hospital. " he stopped as he was appearing to be moved emotionally, when another servant took over.

" sir, i thought of checking other cars also and when we found our leader's son's wife, just like our madam unconscious." We called for women to cover her also and both the madams had been rushed to the hospital for treatment immediately. Out driver Velu took them to the local hosiptal "

The fire tenders and the firemen were doing their best to douse the fire from destroying the bungalow completely but the damage had already been done almost totally..

Under the control of the SP and the Revenue divisional officer and other government officials, in the presence of the media people, the party next in commands, the thousands of party workers,, the fire brigade entered the smouldering doors of the main entrance to house wearing fire –protection covers. After fifteen to twenty minutes, they emerged carrying the charred remains of something resembling the human bodies but not fully and placed them carefully on the plain cement platform near the portico.

Quickly the SP and other police constables cordoned off the charred remains and the crowd surging forward to find out what were the things brought out from the house in blacking colour. Expecting the turmoil and commotion the five battalions standing ready for action, prevented everyone to enter the compound of the bungalow when the cries rented the place with crowds shouting 'long live our leader" and 'police atrocity down-down ' tell us what happened to our leaders"

Within another half-an-hour, the firemen brought the charred bodies of the six body guards one by one. They were also placed near the bodies of their employer.

The SP was becoming jittery when the examination of the charred remains were identified by the body guards as that of belonging to the leader and his son only.

On hearing the news the crowd gathered around the farm house went hysteric and a war like situation developed. The mad party cadres started damaging the police vehicles and the nearby petty shops and the passing cars and two wheelers. They went on a rampage which spread quickly to the town of Shirkali and within half an hour, the party cadres in the all the districts and the state capital started the usual bus burning, looting the shops etc. That was the known normal style of showing their protest damaging public properties and private shops and vehicles –uprooting the trees-setting fire etc.

Expecting the normal violent reactions from the party cadres-the state police took a stern step as they had enough time to prepare for such an eventuality and everywhere the standby riot police, special battalions and general law and order force acted promptly and within six hours the situation was brought under control all over the state.

The CM held an emergency meeting on hearing the shocking news of the burning of the leaders of one of the main political parties of Tamil nadu along with his son who was the deputy leader of the party, besides his six body guards. He appeared before the TV and assured the people particularly the party men of the burnt leader that the state would take necessary steps on a war footing for tracing the criminals who acted cowardly in burning the leaders instead of fighting with them politically.

Whatever said and done, the fact remained that the two leaders of the party which was conducted as the personal and family affairs of the leader while giving a false image that it was totally dedicated for uplifting a particular community who were having forty percent share in the entire population of the state, perished in the fire and the cadres and the party senior leaders immediately called for an urgent meeting for taking further action including giving a respectful homage to the parted leaders.

Three days of after the gruesome incident, the Chief Minister's personal secretary – received a courier parcel marked top secret and for the personal attention of CM only in red ink with several tapes secured pasted on all the four sides. The reception desk on seeing the warnings in red and the care taken for ensuring the safety of the parcel, sent it across to the PA of the CM for appropriate action.

The PA contacted the security in charge at the Secretariat who immediately called for the police examination of the parcel for possible letter bombs or some such thing inside. The routine checking was done thoroughly as it was a parcel meant for CM and after it was certified to be harmless with a few papers and a DVD disc as in the case of the educationist. The last time a similar parcel was sent to the DGP and presently the CM was chosen to receive the letter parcel

The CM was not scheduled to be present at the secretariat on that day as he was away to Delhi to attend an emergency meeting of the CMs in connection with an important national issue.

On the next day when he settled down in his simple teak wood chair, the Private secretary on duty on that day helped the CM to scan through the important mails of the day specially selected for CM's direct attention by the PA an IAS officer grade- having office on the same floor of the CM's secretariat.

After two letters from Central government and a collector of the southern part of the state, the unopened parcel with warning markings along with the certificate of verification by the bomb squad- was taken by the PS, who after noticing the special markings, handed over the same to the CM for orders. He also perused the parcel and after a few seconds asked the PS to take to outside and open it near an open window. The PS did what he was told and came back to place a bunch of hand written papers and a DVD disc.

The CM immediately felt that the bunch of papers and the DVD disc should be related to the burning case of the political leaders. It was exactly the same case as anticipated by the CM .

He started reading the letter addressed to him not in his personal name but to the Chief Minister-by designation.

" Sir, i am writing this letter of confession on my own without being coerced or influenced by any one. You know about my back ground and how a PWD clerk like me came to politics and how i developed my political career. You know my methods of showing protest or dissatisfaction or support or conducting the road blocks, the public meetings without permission or taking electricity from the public distribution lamp posts and other unethical and unlawful activities for the past twenty years. You know how reliable i was and how I would change affiliations without worrying about the self- respect of me and my party men. You know how i used to conduct human chains, rallies on the busy high ways and on the city roads disrupting the traffic causing inconveniences and miseries to the poor public.

Now, my time has come to accept what i have done. At my request several state owned buss had been burnt- several well grown shady trees had been cut and placed across the highways blocking the traffic for hours. How my thugs and muscle men ravaged the opposing political groups which resulted in loss of lives, at my instruction just to create a fear in the public mind that my party could not taken lightly by anyone including the ruling government. I do not remember the exact number of loss of lives by the barbarous acts of our party cadres and how many people were injured by the pelting of stones on the buses and how many private cars and two wheelers were damaged by us. But i cannot deny nor my party shun to admit that we have developed or gained the political strength through unlawful and illegal means punishable by the criminal laws. But till now, none of the cases filed had been disposed off or the people involved were punished except in stray cases, when we deliberately withdrew support or intervention just to satisfy the police records or ego.

Here, i am enclosing the crimes committed by me by my son in the capacity of a minister in the Tamil nadu assembly, by my party leaders, my body guards, how my family members including my wife joined us in amassing wealth, the list of properties purchased in benami names all over the country – the secret places where we have stacked the cash and jewels running to four hundred thirty crores during the last time we checked two months back.

I categorically admit and my son also endorses my admission that we ran the political party for personal glory and enrichment only and in the heart of heart there was no serious thought of taking care of the community which we made use of for political activities only. People like us should not be allowed to continue. Our presence would certainly block the genuine persons interested in doing something for the community consisting of a crore of Tamilians We have deliberately removed those sincere party senior leaders who were becoming a hindrance for our objectives of making money out of politics. I apologize to them .

But we have nothing to regret- i was a clerk with a meagre salary and even if i did get promotion etc till now, i would not have earned one millionth of what i have today in the form of various ill-gotten assets.

I have decided to leave – not alone – with my son. Since my party always chose to burn the buses and other vehicles, me and son have decided to follow the same style in ending our term on earth. But i have not included the women members of the family in my terminal program as they were not party to all our crimes directly. But I appeal to you to take possession of all my properties and other forms of assets as every bit of wealth was acquired only by me and my son. Hence we do not want to leave even a rupee worth of the ill-gotten asset to our family members- which would be the punishment for them for having enjoyed the comforts so far with us. Hence please make the women members to work to earn to live. My daughter in law is a rich person but her father was as corrupt as me and hence you can proceed against him also on the basis of the details i have furnished separately along with this letter.

Jai Hind "

P.S.: I am enclosing a DVD disc wherein i am confirming the contents of this letter along with my son to remove any possible doubt the judges may have in the court while proceeding against the other criminals involved with us.

The medias started focusing their major attention to the unknown force or person and the series of confessions by people who were the VIPs of the state before, commanding unquestionable authority and power. The public were happy and unhappy- happy to see that people who were thinking that they would get away with anything they did were being given severe punishment and at the same time, the police remained ineffective in tracing the persons responsible for such benign crimes.

The CM had to explain to the centre through the governor and the home secretary personally visited the state and had first hand information from the police department, besides state home department, besides having a long discussions with the CM.

But there was no progress or not even a remotest possible clue was found relating to the case by the thirty four separate investigating teams including the CB –CID of the state and National intelligence Agency of the centre who secretly started their work without informing anyone in the state. The opposition party leaders who should have cried that the law and order situation had collapsed in the state had unusually kept quiet both in the assembly and in the public, for obvious reasons- they did not want to be in the hit list of the unknown person- directly or indirectly after seeing the last - son and father-burning case

Every day morning people from all walks of life in the state, would wake up with crossed fingers- whether there would be some incident on that –it was interesting for many- it was disaster for a few, it was nightmares for the police and it was irritating for the government. But the one sector which was jubilant and in clouds 9 was the medias. They were totally busy with the coverage of the victims, their family members, police interviews, and the government reactions.

INCIDENT-9

There were a few highly powerful families in Tamilnadu known to have assets more than tens of thousands of crores; two of them were known to be the richest families for generations and the last in the list was a newcomer –a story of rags to filthy riches- hailing from a family of coolies, the person not even having a formal education, step by step built up his successful career through the medias from the beginning and within the four decades surpassed in wealth all the known richest families in the south India- every rupee earned through political irregularities and misuse of power. He finally anchored himself firmly and unassailably as the king maker of the state politics, without whose support   no political party could win any elections in the state. In return for the behind the screen financial and underground support, the male and female members of the family would be given money-making important ministries in the centre and the state.

By making use of the political ruling power, the dreaded criminal would - control all the tenders, pocket the government dry lakes lands and with unlawful sanction from the authorities- sell them as residential plots, - all over the state and national highways, liquidate- those   government servants- social activists- genuine police officers coming in his way or terrorize   the opposing candidates and even their party leaders , and in short, his modes operandi basically was to make the public, government officials, politicians and even top police officials- avoid confronting him either alone or with the support of people or press or police, He   ran brothels in hill stations, bought big   estates running in loss or lack of finance- at the prices fixed by him , similarly the loss-making hotels, theatres etc. He started TV channels and other medias like the dailies and weeklies one by one just like that. There was not a activity which was not influenced by the family and every Tamilian knew about the money and muscle power of the head of the   notorious family- who would neither contest an election nor would appear before the public under media coverage. He would remain in his palace like bungalow at his Chennai and direct the political dramas, with the only objective of filling up the family coffers all the time.

That was the first part of the   history of the family-for twenty years. Over the last two decades he became sober and wanted to create an image for him and his family and started playing a low-key in all his unpublic-like-activities. He wanted to take another avatar of peace loving public service minded good Samaritan throwing away the violence, the misuse of powers, use of muscle power and other illegal activities to get what he wanted till then.

He did not do it voluntarily but he was made to eat his own humble pies by a powerful Prime Minister who got him and his family members and his gang of killers for money -arrested for various crimes reported against them which resulted in their being kept in jail for two years, But when the cases were taken up for hearing, one by one- with thousands   of prosecution witnesses, the charges levelled against him and his family members finally   could not be proved in the court . That was how he handled the witnesses even when he was behind the bars- he and his family members were   set free but the relentless PM kept them under constant vigilance. Hence he found that he could no longer act as he liked-and at every corner the CBI and other central government sleuths were watching his moves, which they should have done before- the master criminal purchased the witnesses with threats and money-and before the cases were taken up for hearing. Had they kept the close aides and his battalion of thugs still remaining at large, under constant watch, the witnesses could not have been purchased for heavy cash or threatened with serious consequences like the rape of young women, the murder of parents, wives, children young male earning members- related to the witnesses

But the nagging pain of constant watch by government secret agents, at last set him right and he felt that he had enough of everything and wanted to have a change in his life style.

That was when he started his own political party and within five years, won the elections , as usual by violating all known norms and became the chief minister for two terms and thereafter made his son as the CM before his party was routed out without a single seat by a new wave of an actor turned politician. There after it became routine for both the parties to head the state either at alternate elections or after two terms consecutively- at the most. The election commissioner of India upon seeing the trend set by the political party of the greatest law-breaker of the independent India, in Tamilnadu had introduced several changes in the election process which was strongly supported by the late Prime Minister, till he unfortunately became a victim of international conspiracies.

Even when he was not ruling the state he made millions and when the real powers were vested with him absolutely as CM of a state, nobody could stop him- he encountered problems of a different kind- tensions for not able to find safer havens for storing the ill-gotten money- tensions for not able to buy the overflowing properties in the family members name- tensions for searching and choosing the right kind of avenues of investment of the mindboggling bribes in properties in other countries, tensions for selecting the foreign banks for depositing the huge funds – gold and diamonds etc . He lost his mental peace when his family members also started the game of corruption and money making on a large scale through every conceivable opportunity. They added further tensions for the head of the family.

No one expected that the greatest criminal family members also would be taken care of by the so called unknown force or person. But there was not a Tamilian in the state or abroad who was not asking the question often ever since the confessions and punishment incidents started a few months before- " why the members of the biggest criminal family has been spared till now?" Actually the first victim that should have been in the hit list of the unknown saviour of Indian democracy was the head of the family followed by his family members. But reasons known to the unknown person or force- the family members existed but with apprehension and fear expecting punishment at any time. Hence most of the third generation of the family members had left the country with their families under some pretext and those remained in fortress like bungalows in the Chennai were the old father- with his two wives, the sons and sons in law and daughters and other close relatives. The top criminal saw to that always at least hundred gangsters and killers were stationed around the residences of his family members and in his case, there was no necessity for the guards – because - without disclosing the destination, he had escaped to an unknown place with his wives and a pet daughter-in-law.

But the unknown force struck the fatal blows on the available members of the great family sending shock waves across the world- because the manner in which the punishment was meted out was so cruel that it should seal the thoughts of criminal activities even in the minds of dreaded underground mafia groups.

The day dawned as usual for Tamilnadu- but not in the highly protected bungalow of the first son of the leader. He was there with his wife since his own children had been packed to some unknown foreign locations as per the instruction of his father. He was looking after the innumerable political activities as an Ex- CM and the head of the political party.

Only the day before, all his direct and indirect relatives assembled in his house other than those who had been packed to secret places in foreign countries by the master criminal head. The reason for the sudden meeting of all the relatives was not known to the servants and others who were supposed to be very close to the family.

The servants who entered the bungalow in the early morning- as usual expecting the busiest day with several guests to be taken care of – had the shock of their life. In the biggest hall – on the royal sofas they found two sons of the -ex-CM sitting with folded hands along with their wives - but completely dead- with dried blood at the nostrils of the persons.

The servants raised alarm and informed the police and the top leaders of the political party. Within half an hour the place was jammed with hundreds of police, media persons, party functionaries and cadres whose numbers started swelling up minute by minute , compelling the police higher ups to call the riot police to control them if it was warranted.

The top police officers arrived and before that the Asst-Commissioner in charge of the area had made the preliminary enquiry. The police team searched for the other family members and the relatives. They found to their horror that they were all kept in one room but dead. Further probes brought the shock of the shocks – all the nine gun-wielding personal body guards were found dead with shot through their chest and were kept like vegetable heaps one over the other in the very big master bed room of the father and the two toilets attached to it.

The news of death of the close family members of the King of crimes of Tamilnadu should have created a civil war like situation in the state for which the government was making all the preparations but the cadres, the party functionaries and others who were very close to the family, upon finding the death of the most protected families in the country just like that-

41

by some unknown more powerful than the powerful family members, simply remained frozen with abject fear and shock. They felt that if it could happen to the dreaded family- they would be nothing before the unknown person if they started anything in support of the dead family members. Further, they discussed among themselves and decided to wait to hear from the leader of the party who was taking rest in some secret place- that was how they consoled themselves when they saw their party leader along with his wives and one pet daughter- in-law---ran away for fear of punishment by the unknown force. They hopefully waited for the return of their leader to the city to give them suitable instructions for taking further actions.

But there was no news about the great leader and where he was hiding despite the killing of all his senior relatives and body guards – the medias were more worried more than the public, police and the party men. The tension mounted and the bodies were subjected to post mortem and were kept in a temporary mortuary provided with special arrangements for preserving the remains of the bodies for longer periods in the ultra-tech hospital owned by the family outside the city.

But the waiting continued for three days and still the kingpin remained- without reacting- in his secret hideouts whether in India or abroad – it was anybody's guess. But the fourth day sent another chill in the veins of the party men and the general public as well . That time, the news came from Mumbai police. According to them- when the neighbours of the costliest apartment complex in the country- smelling cooking gas leaking out from a locked apartment, informed the police and when police finally broke open the heavily sealed with multiple locking system by firing revolvers at close ranges, they felt the presence of the cooking gas everywhere in the flat sealed on all sides including the windows- they wore gas masks and opened up the windows, balcony doors and only after three hours, they could enter safely and see what had happened there inside the flat. The special investigating team smelt not only the cooking gas, but some other smell also, when they started their close scrutiny of each and every place in the palatial flat.

Since the flat was found locked outside the police never expected anything serious except the leakages of the cooking gas cylinders. But what they found –was –shattering even their seasoned mental strength to withstand any horrors in their profession. The nerve-wrecking scenes in the hall- was the first of its kind –encountered by the offices for the first time in their long years of service. The bodies of three women and a man were found in an advanced stage of decomposition with hundreds of burnt wounds on the naked bodies-where the bones were partially burnt with something- the officers could not withstand.

The police sprang into action. Within a few hours, they could trace the owner of the costliest of the costliest flat - the renowned political family at Chennai. The Chennai police rushed to Mumbai but they could not identify the decomposed bodies. The post mortem confirmed application of a very

42

high dosage of sulphuric acids on the bodies while the mouths and the legs and hands securely bound to the sofa legs. The death should have been the most torturous experience for the victims. The victims were put to slow death purposely. By then, the Chennai police brought the servants and the in-laws of the great family to help them to identify the bodies. They categorically confirmed the bodies as that of the head of politically -the most popular family and his wife, un unknown woman and the second daughter-in-law.

That settled the spirit of the party cadres and the various district and state level leaders of the most powerful political party orphaned by the death of their founder and his family members.

People celebrated in Tamilnadu and in foreign countries as well by exchanging sweets and in some places crackers were fired just like celebrating Deepavali or some national functions. Police secretly heaved the biggest sigh of relief and the ruling CM of the state though outwardly expressed his shock and disbelief – but inwardly he was at the top of the world as his party's chief rival had been eliminated from Tamilnadu politics for ever. But at the bottom of his mind- he was terribly worried- because he was also not clean and had his quota of ill-gotten wealth and cases of misuse of power with the help of a close friend who remained always with him for the past three decades. People said that it was the friend- an ordinary vegetable vendor- who was spoiling the CM. But everyone was asking why the CM hailing from a well-known royal family kept the third-rated friend and why he should get a bad name because of the friend. But for reasons known to the CM, the friend remained and the CM continued his political career without worrying a bit about public criticism.

Thus ended the saga of the most notorious political criminal but the public police and the government knew that there would a parcel containing confessions to the crimes and the whereabouts of the cash and the properties amassed by unlawful and illegal methods for the past four decades.

But their waiting for a month turned out to be a disappointing affair. Nothing happened after the killing of the adult and senior family members. Those children and grand children were still at large in some foreign countries and media made their own guesses that the unknown force was waiting for them to return for sending the confessions of the great criminal to the police.

INCIDENT -10

At that juncture, the morning news paper edition of the leading English paper brought shock waves to the public, police, government, the politicians, cine actors and the holy men of the country and the world at large

FINAL WARNING TO VIP CRIMINALS –CONFESS AND SURRENDER WEALTH –OR FACE PUNISHMENT

Under the heading in the front page, a brief summary of the people who managed to escape punishment from the law and the people but who had to be punished for the heinous crimes they had committed without facing any protests or opposition and counter attacks.

In the next paragraph- easy to understand - guidelines were given in simple English to all those who were listed as to what they should do step by step after reading the warning in the paper, within seven days. The names of the VIPs were given one by one along with special remarks in some cases, and the end of the list it was mentioned that the next list would follow soon.

The names were not surprising the readers, who themselves wanted those listed persons should be punished and should not be allowed to move freely in the society with police and government support.
But the named VIPs and their family members were frozen with fear on seeing the names of their husbands, or fathers, or brothers, or grand-fathers etc in the list. The usual body guards or those who were always remaining close to the leaders, holy men and actors all disappeared leaving their bosses to sort out their problems and the affected families of the listed parties, looked as if a cyclone specially formed for them- ravaged only their houses leaving unimaginable disasters everywhere. They were all sitting and not even talking among themselves. Occasionally- one of the members of the family would shout that they should have remained in their own villages minding their own business, when others would shout back to keep their trap shut

Some of the listed persons started acting as per the instructions. The two highly paid cine actors mentioned in the list had remitted a huge amount in the nationalized bank near their residences with a press meet that they would pay the balance after their auditors worked out the exact amount of tax evasion.

A few political anchors who made millions so far were reluctant and wavering but they were strongly advised to comply with the warning or else face punishment from the unknown authority. Except four in the list including the two actors others waited till the last day before they surrendered to the nearest police station where all of them confessed to the crimes committed by them – and even among those who confessed – not all of them confessed everything. Sixteen of the first list did surrender and confess subject to real truth and all the truth

When police read the confession notes of the political and religious criminals, they knew only a small percentage of the total atrocities and crimes had been disclosed and still many serious crimes had been withheld. But the high command of the police and the government had acted on the voluntary disclosure of the criminals and started their investigations and interrogations as per law.

Seven of the listed persons remained in Chennai and three from Madurai – two from Tiruchi and the rest of the six- one each from Coimbatore, Salem, Muruganur, Thondi-Chengleput and Tirunelveli. But the religious heads-two of them- did not take the warning seriously and told the medias that they had not done anything wrong and illegal and hence they would be protected by their gods.

Upon being produced before the magistrate for remanding the alleged criminals for enquiry, the police did not face any problems to 15 days time for making the preliminary enquiry. Accordingly the seven Chennai city confession- cases were sent to Puzhal jail ;similarly the other nine were jailed in the district HQ jail.

On the third day after the enquiry started, the seven jailed criminals were taken to police HQ for detailed enquiry. At the HQ, a team of experienced investigators were assigned the job of getting the maximum truth from the notorious criminals who voluntarily confessed to a small percentage of the crimes committed by them. When they were about to start their work with the first in the list, a senior IG came to the special chamber where the police enquiries would be normally conducted along with a Muslim lady with purdha.

The inspector in charge was shocked to see the IG – in charge of the enquiries –generally top officials would not come to the chamber at all- and that too with a veiled person. He saluted his boss who simply asked him to allow the veiled person to talk to the culprit.

The inspector simply obeyed the orders of the chief .

The veiled person- not a Muslim lady as he thought first- did not remove the veil and simply asked the culprit to sit on a chair and asked the inspector to bring a table to enable the criminal to write. It was done immediately.

Thereafter, the veiled person took out a pad of blank writing papers and a ball pen and gave it to the criminal who was looking here and there with suspicion and surprise.

The veiled person asked the ex-Minister " look at me. Now you write from the beginning- the crimes you have committed- the unlawful activities you were responsible, the illegal acts you have done, the misuse of power, the

45

properties you have purchased using your political power in fictitious names or I the name of others – the amount of cash stacked away in safe places, their addresses the total value, the businesses you ran illegally or unlawfully, the women whom you have molested or killed, the people you have harmed for not doing what you wanted, the total values of jewels, where they are kept and the list of all those who helped you in your criminal activities and their share, the amount you have received as bribes without hiding a single transaction. O K "

The ex shook his head vigorously as if he was a child before a mother. He looked suddenly cheerful and childish. He started writing in right earnest, when the veiled person advised him to give serial number and separate each crime with heading.

The work took nearly two hours for the criminal to complete under the constant guidance of the veiled person- the police team including the inspector and the IG were all simply watching –while IG was sitting- others were standing all the time.

Once the work entrusted to the criminal was completed to the satisfaction of the veiled person, the culprit was asked to get up and sit at the corner of the big enquiry chamber and take rest.

Thereafter one by one the veiled person asked the inspector to bring the other six remanded prisoners who were also subjected to the same treatment like the ex-minister. In between food /tea were served to the IG and the veiled person along with the enquiry police team and the remanded prisoners.

It took nearly nine hours thirty minutes for the all the seven alleged criminals to write the revised confession notes in the presence of the IG and the police enquiry team.

It was night 8 pm when the last one completed the writing of his crimes. Out of the seven, five were ex-ministers, one was rogue-turned businessman, one was a trustee of a religious centre..

Those who were there in the chamber were appearing to be in trance and not knowing what was happening though their eyes and ears were open. For all practical purposes, they were physically present and mentally absent. That included the seven alleged criminals also.

The seven persons who had completed their writing exercises, were asked to stand up in a queue with their back to the chamber wall by the veiled person

He then asked the IG to give his service revolver to the inspector after checking whether it was fully loaded. The IG did what he was told. He was then asked to hand over the same to the inspector who was also asked to check his own service revolver whether it was fully loaded. Once it was done, the veiled person, asked the police constables present to close the chamber door firmly.

Thereafter the IG and others were asked to go back to the opposite wall and stand far away from the prisoners. The veiled person asked the inspector and the IG to use their mobile cameras to shoot the scene recording the statements of the criminals clearly.

The veiled person asked all the seven criminals to repeat what he was saying – " we have committed grave crimes. We deserve death sentence only. We want to be shot dead. Our death should open the eyes of those who have plans to loot the country in the name of politics. Those who are being listed should confess to all the crimes and irregularities or else they would also face this treatment only. Long live Tamil nadu Long live India"
Once the recording was done, the veiled person asked the IG to shoot the prisoners who were looking blank and innocent - right in the centre of the head which he did. The last prisoner was asked to be shot by the inspector by the veiled person.

The inspector was asked to check and confirmed that all the seven fell down dead.

Thereafter pocketing the seven confessions the veiled person asked the IG to take him out leaving the inspectors and the enquiry team with the dead bodies.

The IG's shoot out in the jail created a storm in the police HQs while the media capitalized it as usual. Nobody could digest the fact how a senior most IG could shoot the prisoners under police custody for enquires. Even the concerned IG could not believe and the same case with the dozens of police constables and the inspector of the enquiry team. The court had condemned the shooting and ordered for the arrest of the IG and the team. The government headed by the CM was shell-shocked and was hurriedly sending a detailed report to the home ministry of the government of India to confirm that the law and order situation was intact in the state, fearing promulgation of President rule under article 356.

The bodies of the seven were handed over to the relatives who did not raise hue and cry which they would have done under normal democratic circumstances which was prevailing before the emergency of the unknown person and his or her brutal punishments.

On the third day after the shootout in the jail, the most popular Tamil daily carried the confessions of the seven persons in verbatim with Xerox copies of the confession notes except the part where the hideouts of the cash and properties details which were withheld and not included in press release. The net result was devastating- people reacted violently demanding the arrest of others involved in the irregularities and criminal activities of the seven. The media did their best to spread the message that no longer politics was an easy means to make money or commit crimes. The police did their best to arrest all those named in the confession notes and the CM immediately conducted a top level cabinet meeting to declare their assets earned by them in normal course.

The four remaining in the list surrendered to the nearest police station where they had given an unabridged confession note giving minute details of all the crimes and irregularities they had committed naming those who were involved in all the criminal activities. Others remanded to police custody in the district HQ jails -came out clean on seeing the fate of the seven.

On the next day morning the leading English daily carried the second list of those who had to surrender and submit their confession note.

The public enjoyed and felt that at last, when it could not be tolerated any more- the God had decided to punish the guilty himself, having no hopes on police, law and government to save the nation from certain disaster if the same trend of corruption and misrule continued unabated and uncontrolled.

CHAPTER –ONE

It was early morning 3.04 ; the red digital clock on the wall facing my bed clearly showed that I got up at this wee hours after my nerve racking dream or whatever you call it. GODDESS KALI was present before me in the bedroom and I remember only vaguely what had transpired between us. I got up with a jerk and looked around to check up where I was. Next to me, my wife was sleeping peacefully- with her usual problem-perennial cold. It took some minutes to get back my usual self and when I tried to reason out as to why I got up in the middle of the night.

48

Then slowly and very slowly I recovered something from my inner mind –I could swear that I had the darshan of the great Kali who was before me- she told me many things and I could recollect only some part of it-

"go immediately to Annathanur and meet Seshasayee –he is waiting for you"

I have asked-" where is Annathanur and how I can start now in the night- I cannot drive in the night"

"you can drive. Annathanur –you will find out"

That was all I could remember .

I woke up my wife and narrated the contents of my meeting with the Goddess. She brushed aside the whole thing as bad dream and asked me to sleep. I told her that it was not dream and I had to go. She tried her level best to dissuade me- but I was relentless. After 15 minutes, it was decided to carry out the order of the Kali.

To find out the place was the next task. Since the matter was very important and serious, my wife suggested to contact my daughter in law at Chennai whose parents hailed from Kumbakonam and knew about the surrounding area well. It took some time for me to talk to my daughter in law and it took another 15 minutes for her to wake up her parents and enquire about the place. It took another 15 minutes for them to report their inability to locate the place. But my DIL's father was clever enough to wake up their driver who was running a taxi in that area.

Finally around 3 am I got the news that the place was in between Thiruvaiyaru and Papanasam. There was no road to that hamlet but for a five feet cart road three kilometers from the main road. The parents of my DIL also warned that due to the recent floods and rains, the roads were completely damaged everywhere in and around the hamlet.

Despite begging, requests, even threatenings from my wife, I took the car and told my wife to sit on the back seat and sleep while I drove to the place. She refused to sleep and took the left side front seat next to me and we left Bangalore around 3.30 am . Till then I had never driven alone to any place from 10 pm to 5 am.

I drove without any difficulty in the highway to Salem and from Salem to Villupuram and from Villupuram to Kumbakonam. We reached our in-laws place at Patteswaram around 3 pm. The roads were too bad and how I drove so patiently and tactfully- only Kali knew. She told me that I would drive safely and I did.

On reaching my in-laws place we narrated the whole thing in person and requested DIL's brother to help me to complete the journey upto the destination-some 35 kilometres from their village . But Kalyanam the brother of my DIL was at Tiruchi at that time but I thought that he was there at the village. and hence he could not come with me in my in-laws small car. Without wasting time, I started again in my car with my wife – (mother of my DIL was a school teacher and she was not at home and father was a sick person with advanced diabetes and hence they could not accompany)

It was drizzling throughout the journey from salem to Patteswaram. But when I started for the final destination, the rain stopped and it was day light at 3.30 pm. I reached Papanasam and after enquiring here and there, drove on the road between papanasam and Thiruvaiaru. It was 5 pm when I reached the point from where I had to walk down the distance of 3 km to Annaathanur. Many times we had to stop to enquire about the hamlet and many did not know that there was such a place. Added to that the roads were totally damaged and I drove like a very skilled driver with decades of experience on high way commercial driving.

We parked the car near a tea shop and requested the owner to take care of the vehicle. He was very obliging and in fact offered cuppa for us. We thanked him and marched towards the village on the five feet water logged pathway full of slush and mud. I requested my wife to remain in the car but she refused and said whatever should happen let that happen to her also with me. Good wife and concern !!

It was 5.40 pm when we reached the annathanur –it was not a village-or a hamlet-there were three or four huts and a small temple of Ganesha. On all the sides, we could see inundated paddy fields . There was no one to guide us and we were aimlessly moving around and one old man was coming out of a bush near the huts. We told him about Seshasayee in Annatanur . He scratched his head for a few seconds and asked us to go Agraharam , pointing out a direction where we could see thickly covered coconut trees in-between big grown wild trees .

Another half a kilometer of muddy path, finally we triumphed in reaching the target. But to our shock, there were only two rows of four tailed houses-on our left hand side, the first two houses were almost completely damaged and on the right hand side, there was a faint light from an oil lamp on the entrance- to the second house. Apart from that, the place was deserted except us and the house with a light.

We went to that house and from outside we shouted to know whether there was any one there in the house. When there was no response, we entered the old house with darkness enveloping every place and somehow managed to reach the centre open court yard of the old house. There I saw an old man lying on an easy-chair of 19th century.

He seemed to have not noticed our presence and I had to go near him and introduce myself. He casually tried to get up and I requested him to remain there in that same place. He wanted to know who we were and what we wanted and how we reached the place in his feeble voice- one after another. He could be past 75 or more and his eyes were half closed –might be due to cataract.

I then explained the meeting of Kali with me in my dream and how I was asked by the Great Goddess to meet him at Annatanur. He listened with very great difficulty -probably due to hearing problems. After a couple of minutes, he told me that he was not Seshasayee and that person, we came in search of- was living on the house opposite to his and he died only a fortnight back. He was the cook of the nearby Vishnu temple, from the beginning-till he voluntarily left the job and retired to live with his almost blind wife till he died. His wife also followed him within a week. When we visited the hamlet, the house of seshasayee was kept locked- since he was not known to have any relatives or children.

I was feeling dejected and was not knowing what to do. My wife was fretting and fuming from the beginning of the adventure based on a dream of mine. I lost my spirit when I casually spoke aloud not particular to the old person that the trip was a great failure and how Kali disappointed me, while giving the name of the person correctly at the right place.

Then the old man clearing his parched throat in that wintry evening, said something which revived my –no- our- spirit.

"Sir, just now remembered- Seshu- before his death came to see me one day and told me that I should take possession of a cloth covered parcel with instructions that I should handover the same to any person who came in search of him, after his death . He also told me that I should request the unknown person to take possession of his house as he had prepared and signed his will- on a government bond paper bequeathing his movable and immovable properties to the caller .

So saying, the old man making strenuous efforts got up from the easy chair and went inside the only room in the house. After a few minutes, he called me to come inside the room which I did immediately.He showed a cloth-covered parcel full of dust-stinking with wetness due to the torrential rains which ravaged the area during the past one month and asked me to take it.

I carried the same to the hall and tried to dust off the parcel which caused all of us to sneeze many times. He went to the kitchen and returned with a jug full of water and offered it to us while apologizing that he was alone in the house counting his days and hence could not offer coffee or some hot drinks to us.

We accepted the offer of water and carrying the parcel carefully, wanted to know whether he needed any help from us. My wife offered to cook for him at least on that day. He politely thanked and refused any sort of help as he had made arrangements for his food-with the next door neighbor- the only other survivor in that hamlet-who owned and cultivated lands nearby.

When we left by walk from Annathanur – it was around 7 pm. There was pitch darkness once we came out of the house. Me and my wife did not know where was the path that would lead us to the main road. I told my wife to hold my shirt corner and follow me blindly and I treaded carefully on the muddy path recollecting from my memory the onward journey we took some two hours before. Suddenly we saw the light at a distance-most probably from the path leading to the main only. I took advantage of it and walked towards the direction of the light treating it as a lighthouse guiding the ships. Many times I was about to skid and fall down taking along with me my bulky wife. She was on top of her emotions- guess- yes- anger- for having chosen the wrong time to visit the house and she was cursing that I should have come on the next day instead of rushing on the same day .

When the light came closely, I saw a person carrying a torch- and when he saw us he was surprised and enquired who we were. Even in that semi-darkness, I briefly told the purpose of my visit and he also endorsed the same thing which the old man told us. He then offered to help us to reach the main rd as he felt that we should not walk without light on that narrow path infested with poisonous snakes. My wife almost cuddled me and then the three of us started to complete the rest of the journey to the main road-the villager showing the light and we the city folks following him keeping his pace of walking.

It was nine when i parked my car in front of our in-laws house. There was a welcome party stationed in the portico. They expressed their anxiety mixed with a little bit of irritation for having allowed me to go in search of a remote village in the night.

All was well that ended well. We took food and my wife was there to narrate everything that transpired from the time we left Patteswaram till we returned back safely.

CHAPTER 2

On the next day morning I got up at 5 am and took bath and took the car to the temple of Kali alone. There I placed the cloth covered parcel on the steps . Since the iron grill gate was closed, I could not enter the sanctum sanctorum. After the regular prayer, I took the parcel and sat down on the small hall in front of the sanctum sanctorum.

Within a few minutes the parcel was opened and there inside, I saw neatly packed and tied old Palmyra leaves fully with inscriptions most probably made by pens made up of iron- in the olden times. I could not understand a word on them as I went through the ten sheets in the pack-tied with a dry plantain fiber-thread. Since I did not know anything about the Palmyra documents or the alphabets of our forefathers, I kept aside the pack carefully and perused the rest of the contents of the pack. There were documents of properties- might be pertaining to the house which I had bequeathed as per the statements of Seshasayee whom I met on the previous day evening. There was yet another relatively big bundle covered by news paper; I carefully removed the cover and there- I could not contain my surprise and shock to see neatly packed 100 rupees and 500 rupees notes –which when I counted was exactly five lakhs and fifty thousands. The old cook's life savings perhaps and what a great soul to leave them for some rank outsider to enjoy the benefits of his hard earned savings through sweat of his brow for years in a temple kitchen !!Tears rolled over my cheeks with uncontrollable emotions. For a few minutes I was non-plussed. I recovered with great difficulty but it did not last long, when I opened a small cloth bag of silk fabric . There inside sparkling diamond ear studs and half a dozen bangles of gold and a few rings with precious stones.

Actually it could be called a treasure by any standards and I decided on the spot to give them to the deserving needy people, as donations from a great soul. I neatly packed them again, when I saw the non-brahmin poojari or priest just entered the temple with the keys of the sanctum sanctorum. On seeing me he was shocked and enquired with usual courtesies as to why he was not informed of my visit as he would have come earlier and opened the deity entrance gate.

So saying he opened the grill gate and lit the oil lamps and cleaned the place quickly-lighting a few incense sticks.

He then showed the burning camphor on the brass plate as per the usual practice and came out to show the burning camphor light on the plate with Vibhuthi and Kunkum. I prayed to Kali and took the prasads and carefully placed the pack of palmyra documents on the plate while requesting the poojari to place it at the foot of the deity for Her blessings.

He did what I told . I then went around the temple once and returned to collect the pack of documents before leaving the temple to find out somebody who could translate the contents of the documents on palmyra leaves.

When the poojari was placing the old documents on my hand, he looked at them and without me asking him anything, simply spoke –that too-loudly in that lonely quiet place when only the two of us were there – that too- at close proximity.

"Sir, these are palmyra tree leaves and they are very old" so saying he opened the pack and went through them as if he could read the contents.

"Sir, there is one person in Thirukkadaiyur by name Natesa sastrigal- he can read what is written on these leaves "

So saying he placed the pack after carefully packing the leaves on my hand and went back to the deity.

I was dumbfounded with surprise and surging emotions realising the divine presence and power of Kali. It was only She who took the form of the poojari –a school drop out to give the information without which I could not have proceeded further with the strange old palmyra leaves documents.

I thanked Her once again and after prostrating before Her-took one thousand rupees from the old man's savings and gave them to the poojari and told him that it was from the person who gave me the old documents and not from me.

Then quickly I left the temple and reached my in-laws house and told them everything that took place in the temple. I also requested brother of my daughter in law Kalyanam to help to drive to place –thirukkadaiyur to find out the Natesa sastrigal . My sambandi immediately agreed and told his son to take their maruthi 800 – a small car for the trip.

I took the morning tiffin of idlis and sambar and left with Kalyan in search of the person who would translate and tell the contents of the old treasure.

It was 9 am when we left Patteswaram with the winter sun trying its level best to warm the place terribly affected by the recent rains. Everywhere the paddy fields and the farms, flooded during the rains then looked like big lakes with white migrating cranes were flapping their big wings flying here and there, looking for fish with out knowing that the water holes were temporary phenomenon where fishing was difficult.

We reached Thirukkadaiyur a distance of 55 km from Patteswaram and started the earnest efforts to locate the Natesa sastrigal. After checking with at least a dozen local Brahmins in and around the famous temple in that place-full of visiting tourists –some of them might have come for celebrating their sixtieth birth day –an auspicious occasion for the Tamilians.

We were not lucky despite our enquiries for more than one and a half hours. As usual I was feeling tired after the two days continuous outings in the rain-havocked place but the Kali's instruction to go in search of the person without telling me what I would get and where the person who according to Her was waiting for me, was making me to withstand every hardship till then. But I was feeling that my luck was running out , Kalyanam was running towards me from the opposite side- waving me to go to the car.

Heaving a big sigh, he blurted out- "Mama-(uncle) the person is not here . He had shifted to chinna nannilam- a small village nearly five kilometers from Thirukadaiyur on the road to Poombuhar." We then set out to find the ultimate destination while Kalyanam wasbeaming with happiness as if he had achieved a big victory of the sort.

I was sitting next to him quietly thanking Kali for solving the problems faced by at the crucial time and making me not to give up the mission on some pretext.

When we reached the village- no- two kilometers to the village- the nearest point from where we had to walk on the slushy muddy path to reach the village proper surrounded on all sides by the rain water. the leather strap of the Kalyanam's chappal broke into two pieces and he had to walk with bare foots caring the pair of chappals in his left hand. I apologized for having brought him to that place and made to suffer for no fault of him. With his usual laugh he brushed aside my formal talk and asked me to be careful while walking on rain-affected muddy paths of villages.

The village bore the brunt of the recent floods and rains. Every house appeared to be ready for collapse at any moment with greenish patch of algae/fungi- and the walls were wet even after the rains stopped over a week.

Kalyanam as usual overlook me due to the advantage of his age and slim body- and started enquiring about Natesa sastrigal. His third knock on one of the low-tailed very old fashioned and almost totally damaged-even without the contributions of recent rains –brought the desired results. He waved me and asked me to climb the few steps to the entrance of the house.

We went through a dark place between the entrance and the inside big open verandah. There we met an old lady around seventy plus- who asked us to sit down on the floor .She then went inside the entrance to the backyards announcing our presence to the person whom we came in search of.

After ten minutes, an old man clad in a towel, came through the backyard entrance watching his steps carefully-while walking towards us.

"Who are you both and what do you want ?" he kept his right hand over his eyes to get a clear picture of us –preventing the mid afternoon sunlight from disturbing his vision.
I introduced myself and Kalyanam and told him everything briefly till I was asked by uneducated poojari asking me to meet him.

He looked startled by my revelations and immediately called his wife to come out - from somewhere in the house. When she did – and slowly emerged from another entrance, he narrated what I told him- abridging my report still further . The lady of the house was also flabbergasted , she put her right hand first finger on her mouth, sending a "Ohhhh" sound.

He then said many times sorry and expressing his inability to help me in translating the documents as he had almost lost his eyesight. With a sigh he said that it was his own fault in not removing the cataract at the right time thinking that no disease could attack him –as he was maintaining a flawless health conditions from the beginning- without any bad habits.

Again I felt that another obstacle in the way of solving the problem on hand- get the translation of the Palmyra documents had sprung up unexpectedly.

I requested him with a little bit of disappointment whether at least he could see the documents –which he agreed and took the pack from me and went through the ten Palmyra leaves one after another.

He looked at me expressing his inability through his cataract eyes. I was all most felt that the project had come to an end and all my efforts till then were futile exercise and m y wife was correct-which she was claiming to be always.

Just then, I saw him going through the leaves again-by showing them in the sunlight from the open verandah.

I saw his face brightening up suddenly and he shouted aloud- like a child- " sir, I can read them- I can read them- me –not able to read for many years now- how I am able to read every word of this old document- may be 1000 years old – I don't know sir"

He took some time to read all the pages- one by one while me and Kalyanam were watching him eagerly and anxiously. His wife was waiting to hear from her husband by holding one of the wooden pillars supporting the verandah.

"sir, I have gone through everything –but what I cannot read is the mantra which is given here in four lines . They looked blurred for me but the other letters are visible" old man was talking looking at no one at particular.

"sir, please tell me what have you read " I could not contain my eagerness any more

"It says that these leaves contain a mantra which only the blessed can read and keep it in the memory. That chosen person should after reading the mantra and keeping it in the memory – should chant it three times – once remaining underwater- once remaining at the top of a mountain- once looking at the full moon- once looking at the noon sun- once looking at the fire- once at the new moon midnight sky "

He stopped and looked at me and others.

"sir what will happen once the instructions are complied with" I wanted to know without worrying whether I was the chosen person or not-just for information.

He went through the documents and shook his head in negative. "sorry sir, there is nothing to say what would happen if the person complies with the instructions "
I was disappointed and did not know what to do further. But it was again Kalyanam who came to my rescue when he wanted me to see the documents particularly the mantras which the old person could not read- which looked blurred to him when other letters were visible and clear to his cataract eyes.

I took the pack of leaves and with a prayer to Kali who had sent me on this mission – went through the scribbled documents in ancient language- and suddenly on the seventh page – I could read –they were in Sanskrit- the language which I studied up to third form –the present 8th standard. I also shouted like the old man that I could read the mantra.

When the old man heard me and saw me with bright eyes and happiness on my face- he almost took the pack by force. He said calmly " sir, I am happy to find that you are the chosen person to chant the matra But- you should not read the mantra-here. Please go back to the temple of Kali at your place and place the pack at Her feet . After getting Her blessings please read the mantra and memorize it as given in the documents."

He was about to pack the leaves when he wanted to see the inscriptions on them once again for the last time to check up whether he could also read the mantra- he cried aloud " Oh my god- I cannot read anything and I do not find anything written on the leaves. They look blank now"

I took it from him and I also went through the leaves. I also saw everything blank except the page containing mantra.

Everything was designed by the Kali and She was present as usual in my life everywhere I went. I took leave of the old couple after offering them money and any type of help they needed. The old man politely thanked and refused to accept anything for the divine work he was privileged to do by the Great Goddess Kali of Odayalur.

We then came out of the dilapidated house and moved towards the place where we had parked the car.

With very great difficulty, we reached Patteswaram due to a mistake of making a wrong turn somewhere on the return trip and landed at our house after three hours of horrible journey. Kalyanam did the explaining to the family members including my wife. I on my part did the planning of complying with the translated instructions- which one should be taken first and the next till all the instructions were carried out. But I forgot totally about the advice of the old man to first get the blessings of Kali.

I sprang from the sofa to the surprise of all and rushed to the bathroom. After taking bath, I took my car with the pack of documents, telling everyone that I was going to Kali temple. They would understand why.

It was twilight and the temple was open. But the poojari was absent. I did the usual prayers and going around the temple and still I could not see the poojari anywhere. But the sanctum Santorum door was open. I went inside and placed the pack carefully at the foot of Kali and stood at a distance with in the sanctum sanctorum and begged Kali to bless me. When I opened my eyes, I saw the poojari rushing up and within a few seconds he lit the camphor and showed the deepa-aradhana and showed the burning camphor to me giving the prasadams .

I prostrated before Kali,unmindful of the muddy floor and took back the pack .

I then started reading the text of the Mantra in Her presence once and when I wanted to read the mantra a second time to memorize it- there was nothing on the palmyra leave and it was blank !!

The old man experienced the same thing after he read with his cataract eyes- everything disappeared from the pack.

I checked up whether I had memorized the verses of the mantra before Kali. I did it without difficulty and realization dawned on me that the mantra was meant for me only and all I had to do was to read it once and it would remain in my memory till Kali decided to remove it from me.

I shed tears of joy for having been chosen for such an important mission in 2010 –when science and technology were competing with each other to find out all the truths about life, universe etc. But at the bottom of my mind, I was confused and eager to know what I had been designed to do with the power of the mantra.

But I left to the Great Kali to do everything as She liked. I would lend my body only and She would act as per Her plans with or without using the mantra.

I left the temple with a lighter mind- thinking only about the six commandments I had to follow to give effect to the mantra.

CHAPTER -3

That night I slept peacefully without dreams unusually might be due to the after effects of the strenuous journeys. Next day morning, with the help of Kalyanam, I took bath in the Cauvery at a reasonably clean place . I submerged in the water- and chanted the mantra verses three times holding my breath. Thus my first commandment was fulfilled.

The next one was complied with at 12 noon on the same day and for the remaining four, I could not do as I liked for two items and could not complete the formalities then and there itself . I checked up the almanac and found that the next full moon day fell six days from that day and the new moon fifteen days after the full moon day.

I did the chanting of the verses of the mantra before fire on the same day evening. About the mountain, after hearing a dozen advices, I finally chose the Vralimalai which had a pinnacle where I could stand and chant the mantras.

On the next day dawn I drove with my wife to Vralimalai via Tiruchi and there , climbed the mountain about six hundred feet above the ground without experiencing any difficulty leaving my wife at the temple down. There in the lonely place- I chanted the mantras loudly and thus finished the fourth commandment also. I had to wait for the full moon and the following fortnight- the new moon to complete the entire assignment.

After my return to Patteswaram, taking food at my in-laws place, we took rest throughout the day and night. On the next day at dawn- my usual time for any long trip by car, me and wife started our journey to Chennai –to our house where my daughter-in-law was waiting for us. The fourth day after we left Bangalore, we reached Chennai around noon and after the usual exchange of news I settled down in my room –but with a change in my living habits.

I took bath two times a day and stood before kali and chanted the mantras three times and avoided using abusive language which was my habit till then for years. I also maintained a mono-syllabic contact with other members of the family; there was a visible change in the behavior of others while talking to me or serving food etc I did not bother about it and continued my daily prayers chanting the mantras.

Nothing happened to me –there was no change in my personality or behavior . I felt that I had overreacted to the occasion and slowly brought down my daily life to the pre-mantra style within a week. My family members were also losing their interest in me and within a month we have almost forgotten the horrible trips to the villages.

INCIDENT-1

I left my flat – early morning one day- to go to my sister's house to see my brother in law who was ailing for a week. Generally, the ideal time would be to leave the house in the early morning and return before the afternoon or otherwise, there would heavy traffic on the roads making it very difficult to negotiate and drive safely to the destinations.
On our return journey, around 11.30 am i was waiting as one of the drivers of the vehicles in the first row, for the signal at the Sholinganallur junction. When the vehicles were moving as per the signal, from the other sides, suddenly from my left side, a big car rushed in to turn to its right when there was no signal and at the same time an auto moving as per the signal veered to its right and in an instant, the right side of the big car smashed in to the body of the auto rickshaw forcing it roll on two times before dashing against the median of the road.
Fortunately there were no passengers in the auto and the driver managed to get out of the auto with bleeding injuries. But what provoked all those who were witnesses to the accident which was caused by the car jumping

60

the signal, was the arrogant behaviour of the driver and a few others looking like rowdies shouting at the auto driver despite the fact that his auto was damaged and he was bleeding with injuries. They behaved as if the auto driver was wrong and he had caused serious damage to the costly car, when a white and white tall man got out of the car and asked the traffic constables who were controlling the signal lights and the heavily congested traffic junction on that stretch of road, to book the case against the driver for rash driving- while telling them that he was a MLA of the ruling party.

Upon seeing the unruly behaviour of the MLA and his aides, the public present at the junction started taking the side of the auto driver and there ensued a bitter quarrel and verbal exchanges when the MLA phoned up for further reinforcement to face the angry crowd. Similarly the auto driver was getting the unsolicited support from the fellow-drivers whose numbers started swelling minute by minute.

Suddenly i felt that i should do something to prevent the problem escalating to a bigger scale. I saw next to me a motor cyclist – a young man- of thirty – watching like me and others. I wanted him to go and talk to the MLA and pacify him to admit the mistake and compensate the driver for the damage of the vehicle and the income he would be losing during the period when the vehicle would remain in the repair shop.

I did not know why i should not do the job which i wanted someone to do – as per wish. But i felt that it was a passing thought and nothing more to it. Suddenly to my shock, the motorcyclist put the vehicle on the side stand and went towards the crowd surrounding the MLA and his men- he managed to pull the crowd aside and directly confronted the MLA to told him something.

I recovered from the initial shock of seeing what was happening as per my wish quickly. I wanted the MLA to accept the suggestions of the motorcyclist or rather my wishes through the motorcyclist and to my double surprise, the MLA acted as per wish and in the next few minutes the case was settled and the compensation was paid to the driver as per my terms. I was standing and watching the scene from at a distance and my representative the motorcyclist was acting on my behalf.

Finally the driver was happy- the crowd appreciated the motorcyclist's efforts to mediate and amicably settle the issue and also the MLA's spontaneous gesture of compensation. Thereafter the crowd dispersed, the traffic police heaved a sigh of relief, the flow of traffic regularised, the motorcyclist did not know what prompted him to interfere and why his advice was accepted by the MLA without a protest and why he should be praised. I left the bewildered cyclist and proceeded to my flat – with my own quota of confusion and surprise.

On the way i slowly realised that the mantra had worked at last and in its own way. What i wished had happened –that too- without my involvement. But i was not so sure and hence i should wait for some more instances like the accident before i could firmly believe the effect of mantra on me.

INCIDENT -2

When I went through the morning news paper, i saw a case of land crab by an ex-minister who misused his power and deprived the owners the market price of the property, was scheduled for hearing on that day. It was a case for seeking bail only. The ex-minister who was a terror in his district with hundreds of cases of land crabs, political misuse in acquiring theatres, hotels, house sites and lands besides murders, interfering the cases of rape, assault and murders- filed against his party functionaries –his staunch supporters. He was not bothered about the arrest by the police and his sons and wife were shown to be crying publicly on seeing their venerable husband and father taken by the police van to jail where he was given near five star facilities despite the protests by ruling party MLAs and other social organisations. He had been assuring his family and others that he would come out soon unscathed- so much confidence in the crime and punishment policies of the government.

With a beaming smile , he was waving at this supporters who thronged to have a glimpse of their great leader while being taken to the court on the earlier occasion. His second appeal for bail was fixed on that day.

I wished to be personally present in the court suddenly. Thereafter i acted as an automaton- took bath and dressed and left the house telling my family that i would come back and take the lunch. They were also surprised for the sudden change in my behaviour after the last month village incident.

In the court hall, i got not get a foothold leave along a seat. But still i managed to have a direct view of the great political criminal when he appeared at the court room as the third case of the day. Besides the high security given to him, his own party goondas were also there in large numbers providing the additional security which only a gang leader could get.

The case papers were looked into by the judge and thereafter the prosecutor started his case explaining why the bail should not be given the accused. There was rebuttal from the defence lawyer and there were arguments and counter arguments for half an hour.

Suddenly i felt that i should go and ask the ex-minister whether or not he was guilty. My eyes scanned the court room and the defence and the prosecution lawyers sitting on both the sides of a long table in the middle.

There were I saw a young lawyer on the prosecution side. That was all i knew. The next second, he stood up and asked the permission of the judge to question the defendant. He was visibly irritated by a junior officer of the prosecution asking permission to examine when his senior officer was handling the prosecution case. hesitated for a few seconds . I turned my head and looked at the judge to see what he was going to say finally. Immediately there was change of expression on the face of the judge who said-" go ahead and ask only the question relevant to the case ".

The junior stood before the tall defendant and asked loudly- " Sir, you were a minister for three terms of five years in the past and were the sitting MLA for six times from the same constituency. Now look at me and tell the court that you have not committed any crime in taking possession of the land belonging to the plaintiff –Damodara Mudaliar ?"

The junior was intently looking at the accused while i was doing the same thing at the junior prosecutor.

There were protests from both the prosecution and the defence sides about the impertinence and violation of the procedures of the court in the junior taking cross examinations on his own.

When there was a pandemonium was prevailing in the court hall by the shouting from the supporters of the minister who occupied all the available space, the accused himself- pacified his men by asking them to keep quiet and looked at the judge and said

" Your honour- please do not mistake this young lawyer. He asked the question whether i have committed any offence in buying the land."

On hearing the minister of crimes talking so casually, every one present in the court gave up their protest and kept quiet.

He then started to tell or rather confess to all the criminal, unlawful and illegal activities from the beginning of his crime history which included his crimes before entering active politics. He gave the list of those who helped to commit murder, rape, take over the properties forcibly, poll irregularities which included booth capturing, fraudulent votes and ballot boxes frauds and so on, under the glare of the medias, supporters, lawyers and the judge.

He took three hours to complete the confession and at the end he gave the details of the hideouts where he had stored the cash, gold bars and foreign currencies , the list of the properties acquired through the misuse of political and muscle powers and named his sons as abettors in a number of criminal cases over the past five years. He ended up by appealing to the court that none of the family members had earned one rupee through their personal efforts and they did not deserve to live comfortably. They should be asked to work to earn at least from then onwards.

I was all the time looking at the junior lawyer who was looking at the defendant confessing to the crimes one after another without a break.

The marathon confession took the energy of the minister who was in jail for fifteen days at a stretch before being whisked to the court and he fell down unconscious on the witness box itself. The court and the people in the court hall were spellbound by the revelations and were looking haplessly at the fallen ex-minister.

Suddenly the court woke up and thereafter the doctor was brought ; the accused was examined and found to have fainted due to exhaustion only. During the intervening period, the crowd of supporters which included his sons and close aides had quietly vanished, right under the eyes of the police and the court officials.

I also left the court leaving the junior lawyer who was reported to have told the press medias that he did not remember anything about the question he had asked. He also did not know what had happened in court

But the media lifted him to the top of the world and made him the hero of the confession case.

INCIDENT -3

My wife was pestering me for a week to take her to the biggest yagna under the directions of a famous swamiji at the Island grounds. The yagna was being performed for ten days. That was the last day and i had to take her by car. It took one and half hours to reach the Islands and another fifteen minutes to get a parking space. Finally we made it to the thatched pandal where thousands of devotees already assembled waiting for His Holiness Swami Swarganandaji to complete the yagna.

Swamiji arrived amidst firing of cracker-bombs; with the shouting of long live the swamji by his devotees the elephant garlanded him; pundits received him with all honours like showing deepa aradhana etc. He was escorted to the yagna area where he was seated near the first pit of fire, There were 108 pits of fire where the yagnas were performed for the past nine days by groups of Prohits chanting mantras in Sanskrit continuously nights and days and the ceremony would be come to end by throwing a bag of something into the fire simultaneously in all the 108 pits of fire- Swamiji was given the first pit of fire, other holy men who had come at the invitation of the swamiji were given other pits as per some unwritten seniority and popularity list and a few were given to the top Pandits of the country.

At the appointed time, the holy men dropped the bag of something into the fire and the entire crowd stood up to shout in praise of their spiritual gurus physically present. The whole area was reverberating with the thunderous shouts and it took a few minutes for the cacophony to subside.

The swamiji then asked the guests of holy men to come to the stage where decorated thrones were kept ready for each swamiji and in a order already programmed the holy men occupied the seats and in the middle of the row, the host swamiji sat majestically radiating divinity all over this person with ornaments of gold and precious stones including diamonds-covering his chest, wrist, and the fingers. The holy men —most of them were wearing the costliest dress —pure silk made and were looking like contestants for a fashion parade for swamijis.

I was standing far away from the platform where the holy were seated in a semi-circle row.

The closing ceremony started and the guests started coming one by one to felicitate and say a few words to their devotees present in the crowd.

I suddenly felt that i should go and ask the swamijis one by one whether they were real holy persons or ordinary persons with all human weaknesnses. But i knew that it would be impossible to even to go near the holy ones leave alone asking them whether they were real or fake. But my eyes fell on an old man sitting a few rows before me —sitting with folded hands and closed eyes. I was looking at that person for a few minutes and thereafter i did not do anything.

The old man suddenly stood up and raised his hands and asked permission to question the holy ones. There were protests from the crowd asking the old man to sit down and meet the swamiji personally without obstructing the ongoing programs. But the old man persisted and shouted for permission where up on the host swamiji asked him to come to the stage.

The rest had already been narrated by me under incident -3

INCIDENT -4

Krishnan was my third son's school mate. One day he came to see my son and his new flat where we have shifted recently. He was studying with my son till the 12th standard. Thereafter he took a degree in visual communication which was his dream and searched for a suitable opportunity to join the film industry as a cameraman. But , he could not get any job of his expectation and finally he was taken as an apprentice camera man for a leading TV company where he slogged for hours doing the same thing again and again. When a new TV company was started he tried and love would have it, he got the job of a TV camera man. He thought that he had put his first step towards achieving his lifelong of dream of a movie camera man.

I was introduced to the young man who was looking very reserved and a man of few words. He did not marry as he felt that he had not settled in life. When he told me who the boss of his TV company, i asked him whether i could get a chance to meet him to ask him a few questions. He smiled and said that it was not difficult to see the boss but asking questions he said that it would not be possible.

He then casually told us that there was an appointment fixed for TV interview on the next day with the boss and he was the camera man fixed for the program . I could take the opportunity to see the boss if i wanted but there should be no questions asked- he made it clear. I agreed and accordingly i should meet him at the TV company's HQ at Ashok Naga at least an hour before the interview. My wife and my son did not like my meeting with the notorious minister fearing that i might ask questions and earn the wrath of the powerful gang leader. I promised not to do any such thing foolishly as i knew the power of the minister and went there an hour before the interview.

Krishnan asked me to simply sit on a iron chair and was busy in the preparations of the interview. Within an hour the place became lively with many famous TV companies crew setting their cameras and checking this and that.

Around 4 pm a beautiful girl appeared dressed like a fashion designer and was being briefed by the senior program executives of the Krishnan TV company.

Exactly 25 minutes after the appointment, the political hero entered the shooting hall- majestically dressed like a typical Tamilnadu minister with long towel –with folded hands and was seated carefully on a throne like chair.

Thereafter the interview started – with the cameras focussed on him and the girl who was to ask the questions already fixed and the answers already rehearsed by the minister- at his residence.

The program was being telecasted live by the TV company owned by the boss but one day before the interview- the minister met the media people and told them that the next day interview would shake the roots of the Indian politics. Actually he wanted to create a sensation and an expectation by the viewing public for the interview. It was only his usual gimmick- in reality he had nothing to tell that would   shake his own party- leave alone Indian politics.

Other TV companies fell in to his trap as expected by the shrewd criminal turned politician, and they also telecasted the interview live.

Bu the questions asked and the answers mere normal and formal. The media crew were getting irritated.

I was standing behind Krishnan who himself was shooting behind a prominent national TV company.

I felt that i should go and stop the question and answer non-sense in the name of the interview and should ask him the real serious questions which millions of people wanted to ask for years.

There were only a few questions left according to the girl who was asking the questions on seeing the minister who was acting he was tired of relying to the questions, already approved by him . Suddenly Krishnan gave the video camera to his assistant and pushed aside the other TV company in front of him and moved across to stand before the boss. He then asked him-point blanck- whether he could ask a question. The TV crew of all the companies were surprised- programme executive was shocked and the viewers of the political party of the boss were also surprised. But all of them immediately pacified themselves by telling each other that it must be the special something planned by the boss to shake the root of the Indian politics.

The boss looked at Krishnan whom he had seen before with the camera team of his company - but he had no idea whether it was a part of the program of the day or not. But the live telecast was on and hence he smiled at Krishnan and asked him to go ahead.

The organisers thought that the boss had introduced an element of surprise by allowing his staff to question him instead of the lady. There were lot of confusions when the boss asked Krishnan to ask the question.

Krishnan hesitated for a few seconds only when he asked " Sir, can you tell about your political background and how you have climbed upto this level of political importance?"

The media crew and others including the viewing public lost their suddenly interest on hearing the anti-climax question by a surprise questioner. The organisers heaved a sigh of relief as the questions were simple which could be easily answered by the political boss without difficulty- of course – it would be a bundle of lies –about sacrifices and unselfish public service and other bullshits .

With his trade mark smile- right under the direct home service telecasting-
the boss said quietly and firmly-
But he had totally confessed to all his criminal activities from the beginning
to the live media telecast –i have already given the details under incident -
4.
I left the TV studio- the interview venue- quietly and before me Krishnan
disappeared from the scene and remained not traceable till now for threat
of life from the relatives and the loyalist-thugs of the Minister who had been
sentenced to death by hanging by the high court of Chennai despite the
fact that capital punishment should not be given normally in any case of
crime in the country- but the judges categorically reiterated their combined
unanimous judgment that the minister with eleven of his aides including his
two sons and one son in law deserved to die by hanging as their crimes
were exceptionally cruel and inhuman. The supreme court also confirmed
and added that they did not deserve even the clemency by the President –
the first time in the case of death penalty in the independent India.

INCIDENT -5
My daughter in law is working in a big international software company as a
senior manager. She got two tickets for attending the film industry's
platinum jubilee function at Nehru stadium Chennai- the first of the four
events to be held to celebrate the 75 years of the cinema industry in the
country. She would not be able to make it as she was to fly to Singapore
on an official assignment and my son her husband also was not in India.
Hence she gave the donor tickets to us and asked her to enjoy. That was
how i happened to attend a program which i hated to do as i considered
cinema industry as the single biggest destroyer of the culture ,virtues and
values of life of the Indians. But my wife jumped to the ceiling on getting
the opportunity to see her favourite matinee idols, the best singers, the
directors etc. She was very much interested in movies and film songs and
the TV shows where the contests for the best singer programs would be
conducted regularly. She did not leave and i could not leave her and we
both landed behind the sixth row- from the dais- behind the cine
technicians in the biggest closed stadium easily accommodating more than
a hundred thousand viewers.
The program was getting ready on its own pace- the film big wigs one by
one entered with raised hands wishing their fans who were whistling and
shouting with uncontrolled emotions and finally the Prime Minister of India
was shown in by the organisers –being the Tamil film super heroes.
The program started with the government approved prayer as the Chief
Minister and the Governor of the state were also present with senior
ministers from the centre and state. It was compeered by the Karnataka
heart throb – an actress well known in four languages including Tamil and
Hindi and a Tamil cine male actor known for making pun of words and
keep the programs lively by his humorous talks. One after another the top
executives of the film federation of India, Tamil Nadu and actors

federations, technician federation etc delivered their key note addresses. The crowds were getting irritated by the statistics and the dry facts of the seventy five years of the growth of the industry. All they wanted was to see their heroes and hear them speak directly to them.

My wife who was sitting next to me was also feeling bored by speeches and wanted the super stars to come and talk.

That time had come – as per the program for the compeerer to call the greatest super star of all times- the Hindi actor- Vijay Mehra to come and talk to their fans who were patiently waiting to hear him.

Then the doyen of Indian film industry and the old but still young hero of hundreds of Hindi movies Naresh Kumar took the mike and the whole crowd went up in hysterics to see their favourite actor in flesh and blood before them. The actor majestically waved at the crowds of fans and sent flying kisses to show his affection and love for them.

I had suddenly the unusual strange feeling once again that i should go to the dais and ask the great hero point blank whether he had all his taxes and had never violated the law in his forty years of movie career. But i pacified myself consciously that it was impossible to do. I heaved a sigh of disappointment while scanning the VVIPs and others seated at the dais and presently my eyes fell on the cutie little thing- the Karnataka actress who was compeering the program.

The great hero then started his long awaited address to his fans-

" i am indeed honoured to be the first speaker on this great occasion to mark the beginning of the seventy fifth year of the entertainment industry in the country. But"....before he could continue- one of the compeerers – the sweet little actress from Kannada films- intervened and asked whether she could ask him a question.

The thousands of fans present in the stadium stood up and booed at her to show their displeasure over the interruption of the speech by their hero. But the hero himself though was confused over the sudden intervention from an unexpected quarters, yet managed to wear a masterly generous smile and like a great hero of films, bowed before the cute girl and asked her to proceed.

The girl thanked the great film star and looked at the dais and the row of VVIPs. With an excuse she blurted out-

"sir, you have been an actor for fifty years and more. You have made millions of rupees by acting. Can you tell this august audience that you have paid all your genuine taxes to the government in return for the opportunities to make money given to you till now?"

The rest of the incident had been narrated in detail under incident -5

INCIDENT -6

Me and my wife along with thousands of film fans were all awe struck by the plain confession of the famous heroes The thousands of fans were looking like people shattered by cyclonic storms- earth quakes and floods – all at a time. Their spirit and enthusiasm just vanished. They marched out of the stadium dejected with heads down and were walking like robots on their return journey from the nerve-racking program.

Even after a week-my wife could not digest the confessions of the heroes and had not yet recovered from the shock. But i felt that the program left many other film industries magnets from the confession spree. While going the film program's coverage, in one of the leading Tamil magazines, i happened to come across a pathetic report of a girt raped and murdered while her dead body was found hundred Kms from the college hostel where she was residing, on a lonely path towards beach on the East coast road to Pondicherry from Chennai. That was the third rape and murder case within a year and there were rumours, according to the report in the magazine- that VVIP's sons studying in the nearby deemed university including the grandson of the founder of the deemed university were responsible for the crimes.

Unlike earlier occasions of suddenly getting some strange wishes, i was feeling that i should involve myself to find out the truth behind the rape and murder cases- still remaining unsolved according to the magazine report. But unlike the previous incidents, i started thinking always about the magazine report and within two days, i had decided to act without knowing what i should do or how i would go about doing the investigation work on which i had no idea. One thing was very clear to me- that the university founder was an ex-government employee who was sacked for his outrageous behaviour in the office- a hardcore criminal with hundreds of cases pending against him. Once a confident man of a powerful minister of Tamil nadu who deployed him to punish his enemies in business, politics and personal life. After that minister's death, he somehow landed in the educational services three decades before accidently while taking over the properties of a college by force with the help of his gang and thereafter till date he stuck to the new found profession but using his underground power got everything he wanted either by force or by money. He violated the procedures and rules or the authorities did it in his case. He made millions by misusing the platform of education while becoming the biggest chain of educational institutions in the country. His prominence in the field of education completely obliterated his past criminal record and he had received state and central government awards and honours.

In order to get the basic details relating to the cases i had decided to go to the Deemed university and collect the data i wanted. It was afternoon when i entered the main gate of the university where hundreds of students were getting in and out in groups and in a few cases alone.

I was looking out for a university employee who could give me the information i wanted. I spotted a khaki uniformed person who came out from one of the many buildings –looking like offices and not like college class rooms. I quickly walked side by side of that person who stopped and looked at me with question marks. I also stared at him.

I then asked –" hello, can you tell me the residential address of the founder of the university?"

He was looking at me without answering when i repeated my question. He said that he did not know .

But he quickly added that he knew a person who knew the address because he was frequently going to the residences of the founder on official work; I asked him whether he would help me to get the address from him . He nodded immediately but said that at that moment the driver of the office car was not available at the campus premises.

I did not know what to do. The khaki employee on seeing another colleague of his at a distance, told me to wait and ran towards his office friend. He was talking to him for some time. He returned back running to give me the address which he had memorized. I also memorized it quickly and thanked the khaki and asked him to attend to his office work. He did as i told him and walked away briskly .I started walking towards the main gate on my way home..

For the first time, i felt that i had possessed some extraordinary powers to make the someone to tell what that person had in his mind and also to make that person to do what i wanted him to do. That was a revelation which made me feel excited. I immediately concluded that it was due to the effects of the mantras only or otherwise, how could a university employee without raising any objection or asking anything obeyed my orders without protest and how could he run and get the details i wanted and top of that , when i asked him finally to go and mind his work he did what i told him.

I realised that i had acquired the hypnotic power or the power to mesmerize others. But i tried to exercise the power as per my wish whenever i wanted; it did not work . Later i came to know that only when i was on specific assignments of doing something for a common purpose, i was getting the hypnotic power to do what i wanted others to do and in the normal times, i was an ordinary person like others.

Accordingly on the next day afternoon i reached the area where bungalow of the founder of the university was located. I came by bus up to a nearest point and thereafter took a lonely auto rickshaw at the corner of the street to go to the bungalow using my hypnotic power. I carefully avoided showing my face to the auto driver before hypnotising him and thereafter he was doing what i asked him to do . I asked him to park the vehicle on the side of the door under semi-dark shade-even during the mid day - of the fully grown up tree.. I remained in the auto and simply asked the driver to go and ask one of the securities who should be there guarding the entrance of the residence of such prominent person in the city to come and see me. He did what i told him to do. Within a few minutes a tall gun wielding uniformed security person was coming towards the auto followed by the driver.

I purposely avoided looking at him directly but gave him a piece of paper and asked him to look at it. That did the job as i anticipated. There was an instant change in him and he simply asked me what he could do for me. I told the driver to go and sit at foot of the big tree next to the place where the auto was barked. Thereafter i asked the security about the inmates of the bungalow and who were inside and where their rooms were and when the residents would retire and upto how long the bungalow would be busy with visitors and who would be the last resident to return .

After seeing the driver of an auto asking one of the securities to meet a stranger in an auto- the leader of the securities – a senior person-loyal to the family- personally selected by the founder- thought that he must go and find out who that person asking the securities to go and see him. I was lucky that he was on duty on that day-at that time . He made my work easy. Without hesitation, looking at me he gave all the information and more than the details i wanted within an hour. Fortunately for me and the security there were no visitors in or out of the bungalow as the inmates would be taking rest and generally the movements would start only after 4.30 pm to 5 pm. The security in charge told me that the founder never used to give appointment after lunch from 2 to 4 pm when he should have rest which was his practise for years. Therefore, the main gate would look deserted at the afternoons but the rear gate would be always busy with incoming and outgoing- goods vehicles delivering the supplies to the bungalow, servants coming and going on some work etc.

He told that the two married sons and daughters, with their children were staying in that palatial bungalow having sixteen bed rooms in area of 18000 square foot built up area- with built in swimming pool- private gardens, poolside bars, bed room bars and children's play ground, gym, spa, Jacuzzi, tennis courts, billiards room etc . Normally there would be at least ten to fifteen guests for the founder and his family. The founder and his wife would walk around the gardens or around the bungalow just before retiring to bed anytime after ten but before eleven thirty.

Besides the securities guarding the entrance, he told me that there were sixteen servants looking after the inmates and the guests all the time. The servants quarters and the rear entrance for supplies were located along with rear compound wall, under the control of full-ledged security like the main gate. The servants used to retire only after midnight generally.

I gathered the details i wanted without difficulty and thanked the security chief. I then asked him to close his eyes which he did. I wished that he should forget everything that happened before closing the eyes including meeting me and the auto driver. Then i asked the driver to take the security chief upto the closed gate and leave him there and come back quickly to leave the place forthwith.

I asked the auto man to drop me in a corner –in front of an electric train station and asked him to do what i asked the security man to do-to close the eyes. I wished that he also should forget meeting me and the trip to the bungalow of the founder and the happenings there. I made him sleep on his rear seat and left him to catch the train to the station from where i took a bus to my place. I reached my flat at 5 pm.

I then sat before my computer and browsed the internet to find out what was anaesthesia and how it worked and where you could get it and what were the formalities or restrictions if getting it in the open market etc. After strenuous search for hours, i got the addresses of the dealers in medical equipment and supplies of essential items for the hospitals and medical centres. There were only a few companies who were listed and they were far away from my residence.

On the next day i left my house after 10 am and took the bus to the nearest point to the distant medical supplies company. When i finally reached the first address, in a narrow lane, i confronted the security outside whom i easily subdued . He took inside where a lady at the reception along a man sitting on computer asked me to furnish the reasons for my visit and whom i wanted to meet. The security was appearing to be tight. I had to hypnotise the two and asked them to do what i wanted. To bring the person in charge of anaesthesia to the reception and they contacted that person and after ten minutes- burly looking middle aged north Indian appeared looking here and there to see who wanted to see him.

I had to add him to the list of hypnotised. There was a discussion room attached to the reception and i took the big bully to that room and asked-

" hello, i want to know in what form- you supply anaesthesia required for operations"

He looked confused because it took time for him to come around to my control.

I repeated the question in a different format- " whether you supply general anaesthesia in gas or liquid or injections to the hospitals etc?"

He told that it was supplied as per the orders- in injections, in small cylinders, in swabs also depending upon the urgency of the application. I asked him to explain the last one –the swabs and how it worked.

He told that it was packed and sealed in glass papers and once the cover was removed – it would stretch out into three by three napkin- and in the centre the chloroform dipped cotton - would start activating within seconds which would make the patients lose consciousness immediately within one minute. They were used for cases where the patients were reeling with pain with partially mutilated limbs or cases where the first aid itself was to make the affected person to lose consciousness failing which the patient might succumb to injuries before proper treatment. At best the affected person would remain unconscious only for an hour or so. He explained everything he knew .

I quietly asked him to get me a box full of swabs or at least a dozen. Since he was under my power, he walked out and after ten minutes, brought a neatly packed box ready for despatch for some order and gave it to me. I opened the box to see whether the swabs were there and they were neatly kept in packs of five and the box contained fifty such swabs in ten packs.

I thanked him and asked him to close his eyes which he did. I made him to forget everything that transpired till he handed over the box and made him to sleep soundly for a few hours. I then called the two receptionists and told them to close their eyes. I wished that they forget meeting me till i asked them to come to the discussion room. Though all the three were under control, i did not know what would happen after they regain their mental control or come out of the hypnotic spell- and whether they would remember my face and my requests etc. In the normal case, i had learnt that the hypnotic power would remain till the victims were under the influence of the hypnotiser and once the victims came out of the spell- they would get back their memory and mental control and could tell what happened till they were hypnotised. In my case, i did not want my victims to remember anything before or after my control over them. The wishes and the mantra had worked. How? There were no news about my visit to the bungalow of the founder or the visit to medical supply company even after two days.

I chose the –P –Day- that was the Punishment day. On that day evening, i told my family members that i was going to Bangalore on an urgent call from a publisher who wanted to discuss with me regarding the publication of my book on harmony in marriage immediately. Though my wife did not believe me, i used my mesmerising power to prevent her from questioning me and doubting the reasons.

I left my house, with a bag containing a few stabs of the chloroform, three bottles of pure sulphuric acid which i got from a chemical shop at Broadway- at 9 pm as the train i supposed to board was leaving Chennai at 11 pm. It took an hour's time to reach the nearest point to the bungalow. I casually walked down the road carefully avoiding public glaze and managed to reach the street where the bungalow was situated, It was a posh locality- totally silent- almost deserted at that time of the night. I walked slowly under the shade of the trees on one side of the street and around 10.30 pm i checked my watch, i went to the big massive double gate at entrance to the bungalow and tapped the door.

Within a few seconds, one head appeared from inside looking here and there to find out the source of the tapping noise. I was standing in a corner avoiding the street light that fell directly on the gates and the security – a young chap of twenty or so, came out checking.

I saw him and his face clearly and i sent a hissing noise whereupon he had seen me- but i held a dark hand kerchief before my face and asked him to look at me. When he turned his head towards me, i used my power on him and instantly i saw a change in the face and the behaviour of the person.

I asked him to go and bring the other securities one by one which he did. I did the same thing on the remaining two- in all, on that day night there were three securities to guard the front gate. I brought them under my control and thereafter i went inside their guard room with them and stayed there without being seen from outside.

I got the information that the family members who were in station on that day had retired to the bed. I It was fifteen minutes to eleven when i made two of the three securities to go into deep sleep using my powers and took the third security to enter the big house cautiously without being seen by the servants. I did not take into account the dogs that might be there in the big bungalow. I stopped at the big portico with a Benz car parked in the middle and asked the escort about any pet dogs inside the house.

He replied that there were several dogs in the bungalow some years back but after an attack by one of the dogs killing a baby born to his daughter the founder got wild and chased out all the dogs to his farm near Chennai. Hence my fear over the dog attack was unnecessary.

I made the security to sit on the verandah and made him to go into deep sleep like his counterparts and i stepped inside. In the palatial central hall with royal furniture under a diffused light, i saw a tall figure coming out from the opposite room. That person also saw me and enquired who i was and what i wanted.

Before he could see, me, i rushed to the centre of the hall – Under the dim light- i used my powers to hypnotise him while asking him to look at me. I felt that he had come under my control when i asked him to sit down. He did immediately.

Thereafter i instructed him to go and bring his wife- he went upstairs and came back with his wife following him. I brought her under my spell when she looked at me in the centre of the hall. I did the same thing for his sons, daughters-in-law, his daughters and sons-in-law leaving the children to sleep but was ready to tackle them in case of need.

After twenty five minutes, all the twelve members of the family were standing before me looking like zombies. I told them to sit down on all available places. Then i handed over the swabs, one by one to the founder and asked him to press them on the nose of the eleven members of the family one by one. He did what i told him to do and within a few seconds all the eleven lost their consciousness. I did not know how long the chloroform effect would work on human system except what i heard from the medical company staff. To be of the safer side, i wanted to act quickly before unexpected problems cropped up from somewhere.

As per my request, the chancellor opened the eyes and ears of his first son and poured two tea spoons full of concentrated sulphuric acid over them. Immediately there was a burnt smell coming from eyes and ears choked me and the founder. Fumes were coming out from the acid burnt organs of his first son. There was no reaction from the father and the son –one under the spell of anaesthesia and another under the hypnotic power. I then asked him to open the two palms of his wife and pour two spoons of acid on the palm and saw the instant burning and there was an twitching of the hands despite the heavy chloroform given. I gave him the used swabs of cotton to smear the acid on the faces of the daughters and daughters in laws . He poured, on my instruction- five tea spoons of acid on the two thighs of the one son and three sons-in-laws.

The entire operation lasted for thirty minutes. Then i asked the founder to take me to the grand son's room -he was the one responsible, according to the reports- for the rape of three girls with his VVIP friends. He took me to second floor and there he knocked over the closed door of his grandson. He was awake with lights on his room. He opened the doors and was shocked to see his grandfather at that time of the night. He was half drunk which i could detect from the smell coming out from his breathing.

Before he could come out and say something, my swab did the trick- i pressed it on his nose and he struggled for some time to stand and fell down unconscious. I asked the founder to open the night dress pant button. He was not wearing any under wears which made by work easy. I asked the grandfather to pour five tea spoon of the acid on his genital organ- urethra- medical term- which made a mess of his scrotum- with severe burns and i asked him to do the same thing on his eyes and ears with two tea spoons only.

There was some moaning and writhing of the body of the young man. I left him to suffer and came down with the founder and asked him to sit before a table and gave him the blank papers and a ball pen. I told him to give the details of all the crimes, unlawful and illegal activities from the beginning till the time he was writing the note, with the complete list of the properties held in the name of him, his family members and in fictitious or benami names and the places where he had stored the unaccounted cash and jewellery. He took around an hour to jot down the details and once he looked at me innocently under the effect of the mantra and told that he had given what he knew, i asked him to address it to the Commissioner of police Chennai and the Director general of police Chennai. He complied with my instructions and waited for my further orders. I then told him to read the contents of the note in front of video camera which i had brought along with me. He completed the reading within forty minutes and i checked whether the recording was ok. I finally told him to lie down on the available space. I put the swab on his nose for longer time-. Then i poured two tea spoons of acid on his eyes and ears. There were only a small quantity left in the second bottle of acid and first one was completely emptied. I poured the rest on the genital organs of the first son and the balance on the founder.

Then i checked whether i had left any telltale mark or evidence in the hall or on the person of the victims. I pressed a swab of chloroform on the nose of the security who escorted me. After ensuring i left the bungalow after an hour and ten minutes to the main gate carrying the bag of empty acid bottles and the acid eaten remains of the used swabs . I could see some lights and activities on the servants quarters- but i took care not to be seen by them.

I found the securities safely sleeping. I used the two remaining swabs on the two securities and came out of the bungalow. It was deserted as usual. I walked towards the main road under the shade of the trees on one side of the street- praying that i should not come across any vehicle till i joined the mainstream of traffic. I spotted an auto coming out of a flat group. The auto driver must have seen me as he was coming towards me on his own. When he asked me whether i needed the auto, under the pretext of wiping out the face, i hid my face and asked him to take me to central station. I looked at him when he was about to start the vehicle and immediately my power worked on him. I checked whether he was under my control by asking him to stop once and start again. He did without any question-simple obedience to the effect of mantra.

I was inwardly getting the feeling of some great achievement in life- what the government and what the law could not do to a treacherous criminal and his unruly sons , daughters and in-laws, at last the supreme power of Kali did- by giving them the punishment which they deserved - through me with the help of others who were not knowing that they were indirectly responsible for enforcing the natural law of crime and punishment. It should become clear to all in the state if not in the entire nation that no one could escape from the punishment for their crimes. I thanked Kali for involving me in this exercise and i was in jubilant mood though what i had done was the worst crimes according to the Indian penal code.

The rest of what happened after i left the bungalow i have given in detail under incident -6

Note:

Normally i am a timid and law abiding person, never involved in any public activity till now . I have never committed any offence even under traffic rules and always a stickler for time. But i am always intolerant of those who take law in their hands, treat their servants mercilessly, show arrogance of wealth and power in public places, violate law, the rules and regulation. I never liked holy men and the politicians, professional cricketer or tennis or chess player who have minted money out of the sports, i hate those who have commercialised the education, medical profession, divinity and sports. I detest the film actors and the movie industry which was the main cause for the destroying the traditional values and virtues of Indians – particularly those who were born after 1970 in the country.

But what surprises me to find that i have been selected to punish those who have escaped punishment in the normal legal process. I have committed heinous crime of removing the eye sight and the hearing power ,in addition to prevent the functioning of the limbs of the members of the family- who were living happily without a fear of punishment for the crimes they had committed with impunity. I am frightened to think about what i had done to the family members. But i felt that i was not only instrumental in carrying out the punishment and it is for the unknown force which has empowered me to carry out its orders, providing me the necessary powers-without my asking.

INCIDENT 7

The daily news paper contained a piece of news about the final hearing of the case against the head of a religious body on the following day at High court Chennai. The case was six years old and after hundreds of hearings-with hundreds of witnesses turning hostile excluding a few who died- the murder case against the leader of the religious body was almost escaping from the crime he was reported to have committed with paid killers with the help of his disciples .It was a sensation for some time and the holy man was arrested and remained in the jail for some time when his repeated

76

appeals for bail finally succeeded and he came out and was reportedly doing his best to dissuade the witnesses either by threatening or by cash compensation. Whatever it was, the case was likely to be dismissed for want of clear evidence.

When i completed the reading the news paper, i suddenly felt that i should do something to see that the culprit did not escape the punishment for the heinous crime he was reported to have committed despite being a holy man of international repute.

I had decided to be personally present when the hearing scheduled for hearing on the following day.

Accordingly under some pretext i left my house. Now a days it has become very easy for me to make my family members to accept the purpose of my visit with the power of mantra. I could do it only when i was going out for some social cause and not for personal errands. At the court yard, apart from the normal crowd, hundreds of devotees of the holy man were present waiting for their spiritual guru – at the High court ! what a shame for the religion and the religious guru!

His holiness case was posted as the first one as there was personal request to the court officials by some of the influential men who were also the staunch devotees of the holy spirit. The court had obliged and the guru arrived with his paraphernalia .

He was made to stand in the box and the cross examination started. He was the last one to be examined as the case which was hanging on for six years- had reached the final stage. When the usual proceedings were going on, i could get a place standing at one of the thresholds of the big court hall. I wished that the holy man came out frankly telling what had happened and how the prohit of the temple was murdered and by whom to the best of his knowledge.

I looked intently at the holy man looking like god-incarnation- with eyes radiating divinity and body language speaking volumes about his holiness personification. I felt that the swamiji was brought under my power. But it was confirmed within a few seconds when the holy man instead of replying to the routine meaningless questions of the stage managed hearing, started blurting out –

" your honour- enough is enough- the case is being dragged on for years . I would like to come out open and admit my guilt in this case." Those present in the court room stood up with shock. The judge himself was rattled.

" Sir, your honour, i was responsible for the murder of the poor prohit Varadarajan . He came once to see me after Nine in the night to get my appointment and direction for the forthcoming temple festival. It was raining heavily outside and he managed to reach the ashram only at around 10 pm. My disciples had retired to their quarters. The ashram security on seeing the prohit let him in but told him that the i might have gone to rest room, But the prohit convinced him that it was me who asked him to meet him on that day night. I forgot the appointment with the prohit inadvertently

77

or otherwise he would have alive today" the holy soul stopped for a few seconds before continuing -

" When he saw no one inside the main pooja hall- knowing the place very well, he told me- later when i met him- that he simply wanted to knock the door of my rest room for permission to enter- but what really happened was quite shocking to him. The door opened automatically as it was not locked inside and there he had seen me over a woman devotee on the floor" When he cried 'siva siva " i turned my head to see the prohit who was stupefied to see the holy spirit- that is –me over another ordinary spirit- the woman devotee.

The prohit left my room in a hurry and i fired the lady for having been so callous not to lock the door inside. I then asked her to get out and stay at the devotees place adjacent to the general dining hall and was awake without knowing what to do till the early morning. On the next day , i cancelled all my engagements and was remaining in my rest room. My disciples knew my weaknesses and they pestered to tell them why i was looking pale and agitated.

At last i shared the shocking news with the senior most disciple who told me not to worry as he would go as an emissary to the prohit to make him understand at any cost. He did try but the prohit refused to see him or talk to him. He returned and reported the results and i tried to see the prohit which also turned out to be a failure. Between me and my principal disciple the issue was becoming a night mare as it would tarnish the image of the ashram and the devotees all over the world would spit on me and, my ashram. I had no other go to decide to eliminate the only witness to the ugly act while deciding not to turn to the side of women thence forth. To decide was easy but being a holy man how could i go about doing the act of elimination. There came the help of a devotee who treated me as god and the symbol of luck . I called him and he came running to see me. I casually told him that i had some one threatening to expose me with a false charge of molestation of a woman. He immediately got tensed and raging with anger demanded to know who that unholy person casting aspersions on his guru. I asked him to talk to my principal disciple and between the two, the plan was prepared and the devotee engaged killer for money to complete the job of silencing the unholy prohit permanently. Accordingly the poor holy prohit was brutally murdered when he was about to leave the temple after completing the last service to the principal deity. I did not want to hear anything about the plan or execution and hence i did not take interest in the crime though i was instrumental for the crime. But there is god- which did the right thing- the police while making enquiries unearthed startling evidences of the late night visit of the prohit to my ashram and running back in the running after sometime from the ashram without worrying about the heavy rain according to the security and some other witnesses like some shop keepers who were awake at that time. Besides the wife of prohit came out with the real truth about my affair with a woman- the prohit fearing that he would be taken into task by me- must have disclosed what he had seen on that night. I was arrested and the police inspector was clever enough to trace the killing to a gang and the devotee a criminal turned business man- who helped us to entrust the job of killing to the mercenaries.

Now i have told everything about the case- except our efforts for the six years to pay for the witnesses and the wife and family members of the slain prohit. I told my principal disciple to compensate the ill-effects of my crime by making very large settlement package with the witnesses including the direct dependents of the prohit. Initially they refused to see us leave along accepting our financial help. Gradually on seeing the witnesses turning hostile, the death of the inspector, the change of government, the disinterest of the police in the case and the support still extended by the rich and the powerful to me, they also were silenced with a big chunk of money which the prohit would not have earned even if he were to be alive and work in a temple till his retirement.

I think – i have not left out any detail relating to the case. Your honour- the weakness which a holy man should not have – resulted in ruining my religious career. I unconditionally admit that i was responsible for killing an innocent holy man doing pooja to god throughout the day till his death. I know that the government and your honour would certainly punish me now or later. But there should be no more waiting for giving the punishment – hence, " he stopped and from his long towel which he normally worn as per the tradition- a small box. He opened it with some difficulty and before those who were present, including me – could guess what was going to happen- he swallowed some tablet like thing. That was all- the holy spirit fell down- later pronounced as dead due cyanide poison.

I felt gratified to see the end of an unholy man but i never expected that he always carried with him the cyanide pills like the Tamil Tigers of Eelam and punished himself after a hypnotised confession i never wished him to die but it had happened beyond my control and wish .How ? i felt that the mantra had other powers as well and it was capable of acting on its own also.

INCIDENT-8

I was returning from a visit to my Kali temple near Kumbakonam via Myladuthurai in my car along with my wife and my daughter-in-law when near the Sirkahli town, there was traffic jam. Vehicles could neither get out or get in to the town. Upon enquiry i found the political party run by a family of son and father known for violence and fickle mindedness- frequently changing alliances just to remain in power always, while burning buses and private vehicles in every political agitation organised by them- besides blocking the roads with trees mercilessly cut for obstructing the high ways and stopping the train services- regularly.

The party leader and his son always remained without party positions and for formality sake, their trusted lieutenants were given the top posts of president and general secretary of the party but in reality the son and father combination only ran the party and its nefarious political activities. Invariably one or two members of the party would be given ministerial posts by the ruling party. The father and son were making use of the posts to earn for themselves in the name of uplifting or serving the people belonging to his community which constituted 40% of the total population of the state. The founder was a just a PWD clerk and during an agitation for demanding a reservation for his community people, he used the tactics of cutting the trees and laying them across the highways to stop the traffic, which produced the results. He was allowed to talk to the government officers on behalf of the local people . When he found that his new avatar gave him a leader status and publicity – he took advantage and formed a communal party to get reservations in government services, elections and educational institutions. He conducted several agitations and paralysed the traffic and the government machinery by calling bandhs in the four districts where the people from his community were in large numbers. In course of time, he lived at Sirkahli in his farm house and directed the activities of his communal party. Ruling party and the Chief Ministers showed him respect and called on him before election. Within five years, he became a king maker and people thronged his farm house seeking his recommendation for contesting the elections. That gave the idea why he should not start his own political party representing the largest community of the state. He started the party on an auspicious day- in the main hall of his farm house. Within a short period of five years, the party boasted of a membership of ten million people and hence, no political party could ever think of getting the minimum number of members in the assembly without the support of the Sirkhali communal based party founded by the father and run by the father and son off late.

I knew about the political party. I was treated with no seriousness by the educated section of his own community. He was somehow able to hoodwink the poor and the working class belonging to his community and that was how he was able to survive as a political party also.

I had decided to punish the father and son for the crimes they had committed with impunity till now. They must have burnt at least a hundred buses and many number of private vehicles besides, involving in the killing of innocent on-lookers by barbarous acts of his party cadres who usually go berserk during agitations by attacking passers-by and passengers of trains and buses, besides the shop keepers.

I had decided to come back again and take care of the family in an organised manner

A few days after i returned to Chennai i gave some cock and bull story, left Chennai carrying my bag- containing two bottles of acid and one pack of chloroform swabs. I took a bus from Koyambedu and reached Myladuthurai in the morning . I got a room in a small hotel just to use the bath room only. I took breakfast and then took a bus to SIrkahli – 25 Km from Myladuthurai town. I remained as if i was sleeping with my usual kerchief covering the face act. AT Sirkhali- i walked around like a business man seriously looking at the shops etc. When it was eleven in the morning, i called an auto and within a few seconds brought him under my spell. I then asked him to take me to the farm house of the famous political leader- on the outskirts of the town. There i asked him to park the scooter at a distance. I saw lot of people – might be party me- functionaries roaming around – with a number of cars parked near the gate. I saw an elderly person- standing alone- with white and white political party uniform of Tamilnadu. I asked the auto driver to tell the person to meet me. The old man was surprised but followed the driver to the auto. Without seeing him, i asked him to look at me which he did. I wished that he should obey me which he did.

I asked the driver to go to sleep with a promise that i would wake him when required. He sat down under the shady of a big tamarind tree and instantly slept. That was the power of the mantra- i felt. Thereafter i grilled the old man to tell me about the normal activities of the founder, his son, when they would come to the farm house, how long they would stay there- who were the other inmates of the house, what about the security arrangements etc. He told whatever he knew but that was not sufficient for me During the interview, i did not allow him to see my face once. When i found that he was no longer needed, i asked him who knew about what i asked. He told clearly that one Rathnam who always remained with the party boss and his family knew all the details i wanted. I asked him whether he could go and bring that person to me. He said that he would try. But i felt that it was not advisable . Hence i asked him whether he knew where Rathinam lived. His reply was disappointing. The person under reference stayed always with the founder only. But the additional information given by him helped. That Rathnam used to visit his relative in North Mada street. He agreed to take me to the relative house. But that could raise the eye brows of others who had come with him. Then only asked who he was. He said that he was a business man - wanted some favours done by the government department in his native place at Adhuthurai – a medium village- 40 km from sirkhali and hence he had brought the party functionaries of his village to talk to the founder on his behalf .

I asked him to go back to his car and go to sleep forgetting everything he said and saw. I woke up the auto driver and asked him to escort the old man to his car and see that he lied down on the back seat and go to sleep immediately.

I left the farm house area and went to the North mada street house of the relative of the close aide of the founder. I stopped the vehicle and got out with wiping my face with kerchief to avoid being seen by any one. The house was open and one old lady was sitting outside chewing betel leaves and a few inmates were talking loudly inside.

I saw the lady and she had seen me- with her cataract infected eyes. I mesmerised her and asked her whether Rathinam was inside. She immediately shouted the name looking inside the house. I hid my face with the kerchief as if i was sweating under the afternoon sun and saw through my finders two male members came out. One must be the man i wanted. I asked who was rathinam. The one with a full hand white shirt answered my question in affirmative and i hypnotised both of them by suddenly looking at them intently. They folded up which i came to know confidently when they both down on the floor upon my request.

I asked the other male member and the old lady to go inside and sleep. They immediately left me and Rathinam alone- the old lady taking her own time to get up and leave us alone.

I asked him about the time when and where the family members of the founder would go to sleep- about the dogs if any inside the house- when the servants would retire- who besides the securities were engaged in protecting the families- how long would founder remain in the farm- whether his son was present now and other details i could not get from the old man.

He replied point by point – clearly and once my purpose was over, i asked him to forget everything about my visit and what i asked him and others and go to sleep deeply.

I quietly returned to waiting auto and asked the auto driver to drop me near a lonely place near the bus stand. I told the auto driver to forget what he had heard or seen till then and made him to sleep deeply .

I boarded the bus to Myladuthurai and reached my cheap hotel room and rested. Around five thirty in the evening, i vacated the room, and boarded a bus to Sirkali. Within thirty minutes i got down at the bus stand of the town. I searched for a theatre and very near the bus stand there was a theatre. Without seeing what movie was, i purchased the costliest ticket . The show has just started and i managed to find my seat in the semi-darkness. There were only four or five persons including me which meant that the film must have run for weeks or must have been a flop. Whatever it was, i slumped into the cushion seat and wanted to sleep for one hour as i would be busy throughout the night awake.

The show was over by nine thirty and i came out and looked around for a semblance of good hotel to eat. I found a vegetarian mess nearby and i took my time to eat till the employees started the process of closing the mess for the day.

I walked out slowly and checked the watch. It was ten twenty. The traffic was not much. Here and there i could see an auto but there was no driver. After twenty minutes walking, i saw an auto coming in the opposite direction which i signalled to stop. He did but spontaneously told me that he was going back home asking me to hire some other auto. I left him as he must have been hungry and walked further when an auto driver on his own stopped his vehicle and asked me where i wanted to go.

Without looking at him directly i asked him to look at me which he did. I brought him under the spell of the mantra. Thereafter till i reached the farm house, i was enjoying the cold blast from the late night atmosphere. The road to the farm house otherwise remaining always busy looked deserted except the street lights. Near the big ornamental metal gate- there were no vehicles. I asked the driver to park the auto under a shade 20 metres away from the gate and asked him to go and tell the security that i wanted to see them.

He did what i told and within a few minutes, a short stout thug like fellow was coming towards the auto along the auto driver. I saw him and with the usual kerchief trick., i mesmerised him and asked him to bring the others. One after another four securities came and went. When i found that there were no other person at the gate, i asked the auto driver to go into deep sleep on the back seat- he did.

I went with the securities and once inside the farm, i checked up the security room and around. At a distance, i saw some lights –from the servants quarters. I wanted to bring all the six-not seven- one had gone on leave- body guards also under my spell. But i did only for two along with the three securities and that meant that three more were on their duty of going around the farm house. Hence i waited for them to turn up.

After fifteen minutes wait, one appeared and i asked the security to call him which he did. I hypnotised that fellow also. Another ten minutes, the last one also fell. I asked all the six guards to come with me to the entrance of the farm house and asked one of them to open the doors. He said that the door was locked inside. I asked them whether there was any other entrance to the house. One of the guards came forward to open the front door. He said that one of the windows on the side of the house, was a fire escape and it would open from outside. Only he and a few others knew about it. He was the senior most of the six guards and a long time body guard for the founder.

As per statement, he went out and after a few minutes wait, opened the door from inside. The six of us-five guards and me stepped inside. There was small space between the front door and the door of the main hall. It was kept open by the guard who unlocked the front door.

I asked the six of them to lie down and go in to deep sleep under the stair case leading to the first floor. They did what i instructed them to do. When i was sure that they had gone into sleep, i took the advice of Rathinam and climbed the stair case to reach the room near the balcony. That was the master room of the father. I knocked the door with taps just sufficient for the purpose. There was no immediate response. I tapped again. I did want to wake up the son or his wife. After a few repeated taps, there was movement inside and presently the founder- fully boozed appeared at the threshold –blinking at me with unsteady legs and hands.

I simply brought him under my spell of mantra and took him down by carefully closing the door behind me, leaving the wife sleeping. I brought him to ground floor where i asked him before the centre table. I gave the blank papers and a pen and asked him to give the minute details of all his criminal, unlawful and illegal activities and the details of the properties he had in his, family members, and benami names with the details of where he had kept the cash and jewellery belonging to the family. He did it slowly as he was not able to write fast. But how i could help him- hence, i waited patiently for one and half hours before he completed the writing assignment. Thereafter i kept the video camera before him and asked him to read the contents at a low voice and i kept the camera sufficiently close to record his confession clearly for the authorities to know what he had done from his own mouth.

Once he had done what i wanted him to do, i asked him to wake his son in the right hand side corner of the first floor facing the gate. Again the son did not respond for the repeated taps and only his wife appeared. On seeing her father in law she was terribly tensed. But i did my job of mesmerising her from standing sideways behind the door and she was dragged to the corner where i laid her down and returned to watch the father waking up his son. When there was no response i asked the father to get inside the room to wake him. I stood behind the bed so that the son would not see me when he got up. It took a few minutes for the son to get up from sleep by the father physically shaking him vigorously. The son got up at last and on seeing his father near his bed, he quickly jumped from the bed and by the time, i cast the spell of the mantra by wishing that he should come under my control. Thereafter i brought the two of them down stairs I told them to sit in two dining chairs. I put the swabs of chloroform over their nostrils for a few minutes simultaneously. They both slumped with their head resting on their shoulders.

I then woke up the wife of the founder by throwing a pillow over her from behind the cot. She was startled and woke up to see her husband missing. When she raised from her bed, i used my power and she lost her mental control. I brought her down and the daughter-in-law whom i had to wake up to come with me. I took both the women out through the door of the hall and left them in the space in-between the door of the hall and the main entrance door of the farm house.

Thereafter i removed the sarees of the two ladies and took them to tie the son and father firmly to the dining chairs. I pulled the chairs to the centre of the hall very near to the costly sofa sets. Then i took out the two bottles of petrol which i had brought along with me instead of the usual acid . I poured it on the son and the father till they were fully drenched. I took out the match box which i had brought and lit the sticks and in the name of crime and punishment, i lit the two live persons to flames. The father who specialised in setting fire to buses and cars with passengers killing a few in the process, was being consummated by the fire which he used to become filthy rich, a terror for genuine politicians and public, and a leader for the biggest community without doing anything for them for over three decades.

I did what i have been directed to do by the supreme power which gave the power to punish the guilty who could not be punished otherwise by the government and the police in this land .

I then went to the six guards who had committed all the crimes of the son and father without compunction and hesitation. I removed their pistols and kept them safely in my carry . I then pulled them to the centre of the hall. I administered a severe dose of the chloroform over their noses which should not wake them up till they were burnt completely.

I left the farm house dragging the ladies to the cars parked in the portico. I dumped the wife of the founder on the car after removing the remaining clothes without looking at her. Then dragged the other one to one of the row of cars. I dumped her on the back seat of the nearest one and removed the remaining dress. I felt that it was a punishment for them to have enjoyed the ill-gotten wealth till then.

Note:

In all my punishment exercises till now, i used to wear a fresh set of hand gloves, a four yard black dhoti –the Iyyappan temple model- and a pair of new cheap slippers- for every operation. The dhoti was used to cover me while the person directed by me or sometimes by me poured acid over the victims –to prevent my normal clothes getting the acrid smell all over me. Before getting down from the autos till now, i used to remove my regular footwear and wear the new ones. After the operation was over, i cut them into pieces - before disposing of them in one of the many lakes on the way to my house.

Depending on the type of operation, i used to sprinkle a good measure of pepper powder over the site of the punishment to avoid the police sniffer dogs chasing around though they could nothing to detect me outside the gate. All those precautions were taken by me just to avoid complicating the process of the punishment though they were not warranted as i could easily stop any move against me directly with the power of mantra.

The rest of the details i have given under Incident -8

INCIDENT -9

Again and again only the daily news papers gave me inspiration to choose the criminals dodging punishment in the normal course. Today i happened to read an amusing bit of news about the possible escape by the head of the main political party with his wives to some unknown place, fearing punishment by the super force which had already taken into task other political criminals who were ranking only next to him, in the matter of political atrocities.

I felt an urge to take up the case of the king of crimes and his family members for giving the punishment they deserved for their unchecked criminal activities for four decades. Once the victims were chosen, i had to start my usual –facts-finding trips to the victims residence, which i did on the same day afternoon.

This time , i have decided not to take an auto driver as my representative. I wanted a better person to represent me at the gates of the residence of the political boss. I travelled by bus to the nearest point from where i planned to select my escort. The place where the big leader was residing was heavily guarded with policemen, party security men, besides the gate keepers at the massive metal gates measuring 15 feet high. No one could even guess what the inside looked like.

This case i felt was not an easy one. I had to do lot of work and bring lot of people to complete my mission. I waited at a distance from the entry to the street which had been blocked by the sentries. As expected by me- i saw a police jeep was coming towards the street. I thought that i must act and act very fast. I thumbed down the vehicle 100 metres from the street entrance and immediately, a police officer jumped down to ask me who i was. I did what i should by bringing that officer under my spell and thereafter, one by one – i mesmerised the rest of the four policemen who were going to relieve their counter parts as per a shift program.

I in plain clothes went with them and there was no problem for me to enter the gates and once inside, the big landscaped grass covered outer yards was a feast to the eyes. I asked the police officer a sub-inspector to introduce me to the family - as the top security officer from Delhi Home ministry who had come to give some tips for the family members to protect themselves from the possible attack by the unknown person.

He did the job well and for the first time in my life, i had seen the ex-CM the son of the giant master of political gimmicks, at close quarters. He was all smiles to see the concern shown by the Home ministry for the well being of his family. I told the SI to take rest at a sofa and took the son of the gun to go around the big-sorry- the biggest bungalow- with eleven well furnished bed rooms, a play ground like open space at the terrace, roof gardens, two swimming pools –on the ground and one in the second floor in the centre of the master bedrooms of the four sons. There were body guards everywhere with guns hanging from their leather belts. I asked the son to inform the family members that till i left the house, no one should leave their rooms and the same instructions to the servants and others also –just to ensure that no one remembered me later. Despite this instructions, I still carefully avoided being seen directly by any servant or the members of the family, even by accident. The son gave me the details of the hidden security cameras and other measures taken as precautionary measures to ward off any attacks on the inmates. I carefully damaged the cameras and the sirens and automatic communication to the nearest police station. When the son told me clearly that there were no other security arrangements in the house, i came down to ground floor royal banquet hall easily accommodating one hundred guests at a time.

I took all the essential details, including the present whereabouts of his parents- in a note book right under the eyes of the son who had been brought into my power already. I also asked him to give fifty thousand rupees for meeting out the expenses in connection with my trip to Mumbai where the founder of criminal family was hiding with his wives . I told him not to tell what he was doing and not to talk to anyone while bringing the money from his room. Once my job was over, i thanked the son. Before leaving of course, i wanted him to forget meeting me, trip around the house and hence asked him to go to deep sleep. I woke up the sub inspector and told him to take me out immediately. Normally when the son was the chief minister, it was impossible to get in to the house. There would be a DSP

86

and a battalion of police force always take care of the family members besides the family's own body guards. Now that they were the opposition, a team of police constables under a sub-inspector was provided to look after the family as a protocol only by the present government.

I told the SI to tell the son before i started the special inspection of the house that no visitor should be allowed till i completed my job. Hence, i found no difficulty to get out of the heavily guarded residential house in the country under their noses with full honours and once in the open, i wanted to be dropped in a lonely place so that i could take the return journey to my flat safely. Before i got down from the jeep, i took the mobile number of the SI which i required for my next trip the heavily guarded bungalow of the son of the Public enemy one- and after getting down, i took his money purse with a few hundreds of rupees- photo and his Id card, ATM card etc and then asked the driver and the SI to go into deep sleep forgetting what they had seen, done and where they had gone- completely removing memories of me and my visit from their minds- thanks to the power of the mantra.

On the next day, i boarded a plane to Mumbai in the afternoon as usual after giving some cock and bull story to my wife carrying nothing with me - to avoid air port checking - except a bag with couple of dresses and a comic book. At Mumbai i tool a room in a small hotel in business area near to the poshest residential tower of the nation- 34 story building with 68 flat price starting from ten crores of rupees. Only the national and international Indian VVIPs reside there. You can imagine the type of security that would be installed to protect the inmates .

Hence i avoided the preliminary trip-instead i planned the attack at the first time of the visit itself. Accordingly i got five bottles of concentrated acids, chloroform which i could trace the source by contacting the pharmacies and through them the medical dealers of the swabs – which i was familiar with already. That took me two clear days of search and patient handling of the people connected with the supplies.

Once i found that i was ready for the final act, i took a taxi to the posh locality and once near the last lane to the masterpiece of architecture – the tall tower- i found that it was impenetrable and fully guarded not only by the general securities but also by the private body guards of all most all the residents who were swarming around the place- some of them with weapons.

I had to wait and that too- patiently for an opportunity and at the same i should not create the suspicion of any one which might jeopardize my objective. Hence, i was behaving as if i was searching for someone in the near-abouts. After two hours of tension for not getting a break, at last, i saw van from a departmental stores. I stopped the vehicle – just like a police man-with authority. I told the driver that i wanted to check the vehicle and he looked at me and that was enough for me. He was hypnotised instantly. There was an assistant at the farther end of the driver's cabin. I told the driver to tell the assistant to get down and give room for me to sit which he did. When i saw the assistant for a second, i could bring him also under my control . Thus once inside the vehicle in the middle of the driver and the assistant, the vehicle was allowed inside after a routine rigorous check. The securities asked the driver about me – an old man with him.- looking at me. I took that opportunity and mesmerised him and told him that i was asked to come and meet one of our clients and i would not return back with the driver . I asked him to tell his chief and get the approval. He did what i told him and allowed the vehicle without further questions.

I saw nearly sixty guards of various uniforms besides the securities going here and there as if they were guarding the gold reserve of the country in the tower. That was the power of money and that was the power of the security arrangement to protect the invaluable life of all those scoundrels who have cheated the public, misused the power and held the major share of the black money of the nation.

As per the order to the departmental store, the things brought then by the van- belonged to one of the residents in the 29h floor. But my target was in the 33 and 34 the floor-a special duplex flat combining both the halves of the two floors facing the sea. I told the driver to forget seeing me etc and asked him to sleep till he was woken up by the assistant. He complied with my instructions and started sleeping in his cabin.   I told the assistant who was carrying the items ordered in six card board boxes- at a time- that i would help him and which i did at the 29th floor unloading all the six boxes in front of the flat. Thereafter i told him that he would forget seeing me and talking to me and coming with to the 29th floor, and he should open the eyes after five minutes, while asking him to close his eyes till i completed what i wanted to say.

I quickly climbed the steps at the farther end of the flat and reached the 33 rd flat and stood facing the most complicatedly locked front door of any house or flat though i was an authority on security arrangements. I had to knock and i might be seen from inside definitely. How to get in to the flat was the one millions dollar question. While i was standing there, suddenly i heard footsteps and presently i saw three body guards with gun getting down from the 34th floor. There was no place to hide and hence, i took the initiative and asked them to stop- showing my folded air ticket. At that distance they could not identify the used ticket. My height and the body stature added some weight to my claim that i was from Chennai CB-CID. When they came down looking at me- wondering what brought me to that secret hiding place of their boss- i brought the three of them under the spell of the matra.

Once before me they were standing like statues . I ordered them to open the door which they said that it would not be possible. When i asked them how i could see the party leader, they asked me to come with them to the terrace and from a water tank like concrete structure, there was a steel door which they have opened for me to enter and get down to the flat of the boss. I followed their instructions and landed at a place full of furniture, bags of provisions – it was a lumber-cum- store room of the flat. The entry from the terrace must have been a special arrangement as per the quixotic mind of the founder the great criminal family of Tamil nadu. I told the two of the guards to go to deep sleep on the floor and asked the third one to get in to the flat and ask the boss to see me as i was carrying a message from his son at Chennai.

He moved something at some place and the thick grill fixed teak door opened inside. He was gone for a few minutes when i heard the voice of the great political criminal which i had heard in the TVs for years. He appeared at the threshold followed by the guard.

He saw me and i saw him- and he was mesmerised on the spot with a prayer for strong dose. The mantra worked and thereafter i asked the third guard to join his colleagues and go to deep sleep. With the boss at my disposal, i asked him to bring his two wives and his daughter in law to the place where i was standing. He went and brought them. They were looking terrified on seeing me and i was also amazed on seeing what enormous wealth could do to people. They looked with radiance might be due to costly herbal treatments or gold-dust powder taken with milk which not even the normally rich persons of the nation could afford.

Their direct look at me was sufficient for them to be mesmerised and with all the four under my control i was about to start my work. Then i remembered the number of servants that would be necessary for looking after the bunch of the richest persons in India. I asked the boss to call all the servants for me to see. What he said shocked me to the roots. He said quietly that there were no servant except the twelve body guards on shift duties- four at a time. That left one body guard who did not turn up till now and who remained outside my control. I asked him where was the fourth body guard. He said that he had gone down to replace a body guard who had become sick suddenly. When i asked about the total number of guards at the flat including at the ground level- he casually said that there were forty eight- 16 per shift.

I then asked the bunch of four to come to the main hall looking more grandeur than a seven star international hotel at London or New york or Dubai. I have seen them all in the discovery channel only and now i was in such a place.

The time was running out.

I asked the three ladies to go to sleep on the sofas and they did immediately. I told the boss to contact his son and he went to some place and brought a cell. I told him clearly that he should not talk anything else to his son except telling him that he should bring all those close relatives who were in Chennai and other places, should immediately come to the Chennai bungalow within two days and remain there till he told them what they should do. He should also warn his son that on one including his son should try to contact him for reasons he could not tell over phone and no unwanted talks of 'how are you' etc. It was crucial for me to control his talk to his son.

He contacted his son and without allowing to talk, as per my instruction, told him whatever i told him to tell clearly. I showed by action to hung up and he did.

Then i brought out a thick A-4 blank paper and two ball pens of very good quality. I set the video camera on the centre table facing him . I then asked him to give the complete details of all his illegal, unlawful activities, the murders he had committed himself or through paid coolies, the raping history, bribes he got, the reasons for the bribes, the persons who gave the heavy bribes, the land grabs details, the properties illegally snatched from the true owners for a paltry price, the names of those who abetted the crimes committed by him; similarly the crimes committed by his four sons, his close relatives- and finally giving the details of the places where he had hidden the currencies and the jewels, the property documents in his, his family members and in benami names .

He listened to intently but said he did not know all the details as they were too much for him to remember. Then i told him to give the names of the persons who could give all the details other then what he remembered. He said ok with a smile without knowing that he was confessing to crimes casually.

He took two and a half hours breaking many times to think and get the full details. I opened the fridge with my gloved hand and took out fruit juices kept there in a row and gave it to him from now and then to keep active. Once he kept the pen down and told me that he had not omitted anything which he remembered . I then asked him to read out the note by keeping his mouth very close to the video camera which i mounted on a peg table which i placed over the centre table in front of the king of criminals

He took time to read and his reading was worse than his writing. For years, i think he did not write anything except signing the documents and important papers. I then asked him to read what i had written in my note book- but in his usual way as if he was talking to his guards. He followed my direction and his voice gave threatening note to the listeners. I thought i could make a good movie director.

" guards, i have to leave this place. Hence don't talk to anyone even to my son. Wait for me to call you to the new place.. Don't come to the tower flats. It is an emergency. I am going with the guards now and after i reach the new place, you can join-ok. No violations of my orders"

Once the second part of the mission was over, the time for grand finale had come.

For a minute i thought i could use direct method to kill the four of them. But when he was reading the contents – in which he had admitted killing to the best of his memory 14 persons and raped more than 30 young and middle aged persons. That criminal should be given the worst punishment only i decided.

I first wanted the three women to be subjected to the punishment. I gave the boss three swabs of chloroform and asked him to press them on the noses of three women. Without hesitation he did what i told him. Already under my spell, they continued to remain without any sign of life- except their breath. I then asked him to lie on the sofa and put the swab on his nostril and inhale deeply. That started his end of his most disgusting and treacherous life.

I closed my eyes and removed the dressed of all the four and in the name of justice which could not be meted out to the four in the normal course and under the command of the mantra, i poured acid on the eyes and ears of the great master of crimes- forcibly opened by me. I then drenched the acid liberally all over his body particularly over the genitals which had ruined the lives of innocent women, Then i pressed another set of swabs over the noses of the women to ensure that they were dead by the sheer effect of the chloroform itself. I then took out the cotton roll i had brought and poured acid over it and gave an acid sponge bath all over their body – leaving their genitals. I did it three times to see that the acid penetrated their flesh to their burn bones to the police and to the general public to warn them that none should not even dare to dream of doing crimes in any form.

When i felt that i had done the job well- i checked to ensure that i had not left any tell tale marks at the place. Once satisfied, i went to the bunch of the guards and woke one of them to help me to pull the two to the big bath rooms of the flat. He helped and in fact he did the job alone. I then asked him to contact the guards on duty to come to the boss flat telling them that boss wanted to see them- one by one. He did and within next half an hour, the guards reported through the express lift specially provided to reach the floors 30 to 34 . I mesmerised them one by one and took them to the bath room. When the new guard came, i asked the previous guards to go to sleep and thus i ensured all the thirteen packed to two spacious bath rooms. In the case of the last one, i asked him to contact them or some of them. When they came on the line, i switched on the camera on speaker. That did the trick of the job. There were several yes sirs from the other end and once the instructions through the camera was over, i asked the last guard also to go to sleep.

Thereafter, i went to the bathroom and removed the thirteen guns from them. The flat below the bathroom also belonged to the boss but still i feared the sound effect of gun firing could be felt or heard by someone. Hence i thought for a minute and felt that i should muffle the noise. I went to the bed rooms and brought all the pillows and the back rests i could find. I then put it over the chest of the criminals masquerading as the body guards of their kings for years and shot them through their chest. The recoil effect was painful to my hands. But the noise was subdued to a great extent. I finished the pillows and back rests by using them over the remaining guards and kept the empty pistols over their bodies, while taking the loaded ones with me for later use and poured the remaining acids over them after removing the remains of the pillows. I did not want a fire breaking out in the flat.

I then closed all the windows and the doors and sealed the entire flat air tight. I went to the kitchen and brought the three cylinders and opened them freely and quickly ensured once again that everything was in order and closed the store room door inside. I woke up the last body guard and told him to come with me to the ground floor to take me in one of the cars to the city. He asked me about the key. I gave the keys which i took from one of the guards who acted as a driver . The boss never believed anyone else except the body guards. No servant and no drivers- the boss was a genius in his own ways.

I got into the car and the guard who was known to be a driver also, easily got out of the security ring to the main road to some place in the city. I told him after travelling for fifteen minutes in some direction to stop the vehicle near a lonely place- and asked him to go sleep deeply. He acted as per the effect of the mantra. I simply shot from behind through the thick seat- which worked like a muffler. I took the revolver with me and kept it along with four others i had kept over my body in between the dress and my bare body- checked here and there to ensure my safe landing on the road- removed my slippers and took out my new ones and worn them on the road without my foot touching the ground- to avoid giving work to the sniffer dogs - while packing the old ones in a polythene bag which i brought specially for that purpose. I got out of the car carefully without leaving something for the police to track me and keeping the old chapel in my bag i walked blindly without turning back to take a few turns here and there to reach a busy road . I took a taxi and reached the air port four hours before my flight to Chennai at 9.30 pm, with my handbag with the same dresses and comic book, which i brought from Chennai. While on the way to air port, i threw one chapel at a time at vacant places with garbage bins

I took a taxi at Chennai to go to Central station and after taking a cup of coffee and came out to take an auto to my house 32 KM from the station. I had to hypnotise him on the way as a measure of precaution though not necessary and got down a km before my flat. I paid the fare and asked the driver to close his eyes and forget seeing me bringing to that place and turn the auto without looking back return back to the city immediately.

Only after i saw turning back as i wished and proceeding towards the city, i started the last lap of my journey to my flat. When i pressed the calling bell and saw my wife, the first thing i had to do was to silence her which i did to avoid some complications at a later date.

That whole day i took rest in the name of tiredness and did not allow my family members to pester me about my absence for the past three days.

Around 9 pm, i had to mesmerize my wife only as my son and daughter in law had gone to the house of my eldest son at a distant place in the city .I gave her some childish excuse and left the house to catch the bus to the city. I got down in a busy area and phoned up the SI. When he came on the line, i simply told him-" sir, i have a money purse which contains heavy cash and ATM card, with a few diamonds in a small paper cover on the side of a road when i went to relieve myself. Your name and phone number were there. i am on my way to hospital urgently and please come collect your purse with lot of cash and diamonds" That did the trick- the SI wherever he was and whatever he was doing, did not want to miss the opportunity to get back heavy and cash and diamonds in the place of almost an empty purse with of course his credentials etc.

I waited for half an hour and there he was on his jeep alone. Probably he did not want his driver to come with him to pick up his jackpot. The waved at the jeep and presently he saw me and i saw him. That was the end of the freedom of thinking for the SI. I got into the jeep. It was 10.10 pm. I asked him to go the ex-CM's house and on the way, instructed him what he should say to the security force at the entrance and the ex-CM. He nodded his head and was concentrating in driving as his main concern was to take me to the place i wanted.

At around 10.40 pm, the jeep reached the entrance to the bungalow and on seeing the SI – his counterpart for the night shift appeared asking him what brought him there at that time of the night- and when he saw me and i saw him, i brought him also under the effect of the mantra. Before my SI could answer him, i asked the night shift SI to get into the jeep, which he did. We drove to the portico of the bungalow and there four body guards stood with pistols hanging from there thick belts, smoking beedis and talking casually. On seeing the two Sis, they came running to find out why they were there at that time.

I saw the four of them instantly before they could see me after the two Sis on both my sides got down from the jeep. I mesmerised all of them when their eyes fell on me and i had eye to eye contact with them. I told them to open the main door which one of them did after inserting several keys and going here and there- turning this and turning that-an elaborate arrangement for opening the door of the home of criminals.

Once inside, i told the guards to close the door inside and sit down very near to the entrance and go to deep sleep. Once that botheration was over, i asked the two SIs to go to the first floor of the bungalow through the big staircase located like movie houses- with marble and costly wood – one from the left side and the other from the opposite side from the big veranda of the first floor. They went up and as my instructions, woke up the ex-CM son of the master –the room facing the entrance. Half sleeping with after effects of liquor, the son was startled to see two police officers at that wrong time- with pistols in their hands. The liquor effect had vanished instantly and he was mortally afraid of seeing pistols and the police officers . The Sis simply told him to come down. He had to obey the SIs. Once the son saw me and i also saw him, the rest was easy for me to start my mission.

I asked the two SIs to sit and dial their houses to tell their family members that they would be late that day. Once i took the cautious step, i asked them to go to sleep but not deep enough.

I asked the son to sit down. I gave the usual A-4 blank paper and pen. I asked him to write about his history of crimes- rapes-murders etc. He did but was quicker than his illiterate father. Once his job was over, i asked him to go and bring his younger brother who was a notorious killer and dreaded criminal in Tirunelveli town – a deep south city. Media repeatedly called him the king of the district and nothing could be down without his approval. He had dozens of lieutenants who would first act and then only ask. Several cases of murders, land crabbing, poll irregularities had been reported but no action could be taken against the gangster who happened to be the son of the ex_CM. I woke up the two SIs and asked them to go with the son with pistols on their hands. The team brought the treacherous killer son . On seeing him, i felt a surge of hatred for that rascal and that delayed the mesmeric act which prompted that fellow to question me. But i brought the situation under control within seconds and made him to sit down like his elder brother to write his confessions. He took one hour and forty minutes to complete the work.

Thereafter, the two other brothers who had not made any public appearances but who had also created their history of crimes- but not comparable to the two elders. They finished their job in half an hour.

Thus after three hours, around 2 am, i had to start the final act of the purpose of my visit. I woke up the SIs and told them to go up and bring the wives of the four sons as the children had gone hiding somewhere in foreign countries- one by one keeping pistols on their hand ready. They did exactly what i told them to do. Thus within the next fifteen minutes, i had four pairs at my disposal and i asked them to occupy the big sofas after telling the SIs to go to sleep.

I took out the chloroform swabs and after closing my nostrils as usual, i gave them to the sons and told them to put it for a few minutes in the nostrils of their wives, while asking the hypnotised wives to inhale deeply. I waited for two exact minutes and they slumped on the sofas and then i gave the sons another set for them to put it in their noses while inhaling deeply. Within twenty seconds, the swabs fell from the hands as the sons fainted. I collected the swabs and carefully kept them in a plastic bad which i had brought.

I took out the pistols which i had seized from the bodies of the guards at Mumbai- they were attached with silencers which i felt should be very useful for my mission. In all, there were eight revolvers with silencers and they were really heavy and shoulder blade ached while bring them from my house.

One by one i shot the eight of them through their chest at the closest range. The recoil effect was horrible and painful for me. I covered the bleeding holes with the back rests and woke up the SIs to go up and bring from the second floor six guest rooms, all the close relatives of the family members staying in each room- one by one- with pistols in their hands. Once they landed on the ground floor main hall, they were looking bewildered on looking at the eight persons sleeping on the sofas and me standing in the centre watching them coming down. Once our eyes met, they were controlled by me. Thereafter the two SIs would be sent to bring the next batch of relatives of the next bed room, while i took them to a spacious meeting room adjacent to the main hall- which served the discussions room of the political functionaries with the ex.CM son and asked them to lie down and go to sleep. I then shot them through their chest with the silencer gun and pulled them to a corner stacking them one over the other. I needed place for other victims to lie down before facing the bullets.

Thus the inmates of the six rooms were punished for their innumerable crimes committed taking advantage of their relation with the criminal family. I was not feeling any pinch of consciousness as i was also appearing to have been mesmerised by the mantra, or otherwise, i a normal law abiding leading a simple straightforward life could not have even harmed leave alone killing people at close range like a mercenary or a soldier in the war.

Once the relatives quota was over, i woke up the SIs and told them to pull the four body guards to a room next to the meeting room – a place enough for punishing the body guards who had carried out many murders and other heinous crimes for their bosses as well as on their own. Once the four killers were kept lying on the floor, in deep sleep, i fired at close ranges over their chests and brought the end of their criminal life-without their knowing. That was the only concession i had given to all the victims with the power of the mantra. May be, the force never wanted me to kill the victims with their full consciousness as the objective of the mission of the super force was to punish those who had managed to get away from the law with impunity.

It was three fifty in the morning when my mission was completed. Another hour, the whole world would start becoming busy including the servants of the big palace like bungalow,

I did a final checking everything to ensure that i had not left any tell tale evidences of my presence in the bungalow anywhere and then i asked the SIs to take me out in the jeep to the entrance. With a state honours of salute to me and the two SIs, the jeep crossed the big metal gates and rushed into the empty roads with two SIs escorting me on either side. I told them to drop me near a Kathipara Fly over a busy area in the early morning when hundreds of long distance buses would come and halt there to unload the passengers. Once i was out of the jeep, 200 metres from the long distance bus stop, i told the two to forget whatever they had heard, seen till then and told them to go to deep sleep. I then took out the foreign liquor which i took from the fridge of the son's bungalow- and poured the contents in their forced open mouth and over their bodies.

I quietly changed my chapel and removed the hand glove and kept them in polythene bags which i had brought handy and took out the fresh set of pant and shirt from the bag to change my existing dress carrying the horrible chloroform smell. I looked here and there to ensure that no one was watching me , the jeep and the goings on and then quietly walked towards the long distance bus stand.

I hailed an auto as if i got down from a distant place, and told the driver to take me to my place. On the way i had to mesmerises him. Once i was a kilo metre away from flat, i got down and paid the driver, while asking him to forget seeing me, carrying me in the auto and return back to the city without turning back. Once he did what i told him to do, i as usual legged the last part of the journey and when my wife opened the door of my flat, i had to hypnotise her to stop her unanswerable questions.

The rest of the incident has been given in detail under incident -9

Note:

I do not know whether the power of the mantra was hypnotism or mesmerism. But i had been using the names interchangeably because i had no idea what they were all about. I felt that all my wishful thinking while i was on a mission to punish- instantly turned into real actions- definitely the power of the mantra or what else? I have not studied the hypnotism or the mesmerism in my life. But i was able to get my wishes fulfilled by an unknown power, only when i was on the mission to punishment and not in the normal course of life. But for the power, i could not even imagine to approach the VVIPs in the high places leave alone punishing them for their misdeeds. I have seen many movies where the heroes would get unusual powers to punish the guilty or the political person who wronged the public. But that was film making and that had nothing to do with reality. In fact, the very same criminals produced movies wherein politicians like them would be brought to books by the heroes, that was to make more money. But they never imagined even as a passing thought - that one day the movies they had produced would become a reality- and that too, in their own lives.

I don't know how long the powers or the effect of the mantra -would be with me or how much time i have to complete my mission and what are the scopes of the mission. I get the sudden urges to do something or take up the cases for punishment and till now, i have not planned on my own to punish anyone. I get the message from the super power to act in the form of news papers, TV and other medias or from what i see or hear. I therefore remain always afraid of one thing- suppose the mantra effect leaves me when i am in the midway of punishing some criminals. Where would i land- what would happen to me? These questions are ringing in my ears always though i still don't know – of all the one billion Indians, why the super force has chosen me to take up the corrective measures? Sometimes i would feel that perhaps it was part of the punishment program to punish me to carry out   the act of punishing in the cruellest ways. That is why i have been taking extra-ordinary precautions to the best of my knowledge from reading the investigations reports of the real cases unearthed by the police till now.

I am proceeding further without knowing whether i have come to the end or it is a temporary break in the program of punishment. Let us see.

BOOK –TWO

The next few days were uneventful for me- a change from the recent routine life- for the past two months. I was enjoying my retired life- as usual thinking about this and that. But on the fourth day of my rest, i have read an article in the leading English daily's supplementary edition, a detailed article of how many cases of serious crimes remained unsolved and the cases filed by the affected parties against people who were VIPs themselves or who had the tacit support or back up from the High places were dismissed for various reasons. The media reports of the cases when the cases were dismissed were indirectly pointing out how money power and influence could defeat genuine cases of heinous crimes. The same article contained the unchecked accumulation of enormous black money- wealth by the politicians, businessmen, cine actors, mafia underground gangsters, real estate magnets, top sports men, and the commercialised medical and educational services.

That activated the power in me and i was getting an urge to take the cases of all these escapees from legal punishment. But the number of persons to be punished appeared to be in thousands even in Tamil nadu leave alone the country.

I had to change my strategy. The unknown force somehow left the planning part of the mission to me. I thought and thought for half a day. The result was – an immediate action was required to be taken up by me – on the same day.

I gave the usual meaningless excuse to my wife and left my flat to catch the bus to the nearest point where the main office of the leading English news paper was locate. It took an hour and half at the busy evening time to reach the security office at the gate. I saw the security men in uniform and they saw me and everything was over in a few minutes. They allowed me to go to the main building without noting down anything on the visitors book or getting permission from the office for my unscheduled visit to the editor of the news paper.

I saw at the ground floor- the packing section and commercial activities and without asking anyone,, i climbed the stair case avoiding the lift to reach the top floor. I knew that the top guns usually occupied the top floors as a status symbol> but in the case of the news paper, the top brass was having his office in the first floor. I came down and saw two sentries sitting with a phone on a wooden stool and the entire area of the first floor was partitioned by a wooden panel- leaving a small area for the sentries to move about- so that no one could get a chance to see what was inside. The boss was somewhere inside and one should get clearance from several points of security before getting an audience of the richest news paper baron- the owner of oldest and the largest circulated news paper.

To cut the details short, after bringing the two sentries under my control, i entered the editors secretariat- 5000 sf ft affair- with several closed cabins on either side and the one at the end of the long gap in between the closed cabins- i saw the name of the publisher- the owner of the news paper. On either next to him there were brass plates showing the names of two managing director. The news paper was owned by a family over hundred years and might be- the two MDs represented two main families the descendants of the founder.

I just knocked the door and entered the room. But i found two or three officials sitting in their desks and at the farther end, i saw - floor to ceiling wooden panel- the boss must be inside, i presumed. What security set up, for the news paper man – wondered. Before the team of secretaries or assistants to the boss could say hello, i mesmerised them and told them not to allow anyone without my permission or not to do anything from then on. They agreed. I entered the biggest room i have ever seen – with a big semi-circular table at the road side end- running to 20 feet length. At the centre sat the king of news papers talking over the phone and before him, fortunately there were no officials or guests before him. On seeing me he was startled and snapped the connection and was about to shout at me when he was subdued by the matra effect.

I went straight to the business on hand. I told him that i want a message to be published on all his editions on the next day morning. I took out the message from the hand bag i carried. The publisher took it and read it. I asked him to call his secretary and give the message for including in the next morning editions – with instructions in writing that it should be published in the first page- to cover the entire space avoiding advertisements etc. He did what i told him to do. I went out and brought one of the three- looking like a secretary. I asked the boss to handover the papers and instruct the secretary. The matter was over in less than fifteen minutes –the time taken for the news paper boss to read the contents of the message. The secretary left and i had to see that the instructions were not reversed after my exit from the scene.

I had no other go to ask the publisher to take me to his farm house outside the city, to ensure the publication of the news on the next day positively. He immediately called the secretary to tell the driver to keep the vehicle ready as he was leaving the office and would be back only on the next day and all the engagements scheduled for the day should be cancelled or postponed.

In the meantime, i waited for a few minutes for the secretary to handover the message to the chief editor whose cabin was only a few metres from the room of the boss. Then i went out and told the three persons to forget what they had seen or talked or heard or happened till then and to go to sleep. After silencing the three, i asked the boss to leave. He took me to the lift specially installed for his exclusive use to the garage below. There the car was waiting for him and the driver opened the door for him but he never expected a guest like me. I had to cast the mantra effect on the driver also.

We left the news paper office when it was around 6 pm and it took two hours difficult driving to reach the lonely farm house. On seeing the owner's car, several servants became active running here and there as it was an unscheduled surprise visit. A supervisor came running to open the door but i remained in the car. I told the boss to tell all the servants and others to leave us alone for some time. He did and instantly all those who were standing and watching the boss- disappeared from the scene. I told the driver that he should forget what he had seen, heard, happened and did and asked him to go to sleep, so that he could be woken up for dinner in the normal course. Under the cover of the portico and the car, i sneaked inside the house and asked the boss to show me the nearest room to avoid unwanted witnesses for my visit.

Once inside the closed room safely, i asked the boss to order for a good dinner to be served in the room itself. He gave instructions to the kitchen. Then i asked him to tell the supervisor that he should not be disturbed by anyone till the next day morning- except for dinner at 8 pm. That gave the finishing touch to my job on hand.

I asked him to sit down before a table in the room and gave him a bunch of blank papers and a pen for him to write down all the irregularities he had committed till then including violations of law and at the end the total value of his assets in all forms and where he had stored the cash and the valuables.

I gave him ample time to complete the work and when he said that he had given all the details, i asked him to read it out before my video camera which he did as i told him to do. When everything was over, it was time for dinner.

We took a nice dinner in the room and after a few minutes, i told him to go to deep sleep on the sofa which was long enough to accommodate him. The air conditioner was on- i told myself that i should also sleep till morning peacefully to see whether it worked me also.

When i opened my eyes, i could hear feeble noises of the chirping of the birds to announce that the day had dawned. I went to the attached bathroom. Then i woke up the news paper giant and told him to go to bathroom. He did. I asked him to get us hot coffee.

Once we were fresh from the sleep and the coffee, i asked him to tell the driver to get the car ready. I then asked him to go out and check whether there were any secret cameras in the building and he said there were no such security arrangement, except the human securities. We left the room while i was enacting the kerchief trick to avoid being seen by some one till i got into the car backseat and closed the tinted glass doors.

On the way to the city, i told the driver to stop the car at the shade of a tree .I told the driver and the boss – that they should forget what they had done, seen, heard and happened from till that time and they should not look back till they reached the boss's residence.

I got down in the high way and at that time of the morning there were no vehicle movement. Once they had gone, i was waiting for a bus to the city. But there were no bus stands in the highway. I walked for a kilometre when i saw a parked vehicle under a tree and a family was stretching out their limbs probably after a strenuous over nigh drive from some distant place.

The car was big and there should some place for me. I approached the young man and instantly the mantra worked. Once that was done and the rest was elementary for me to drop me to the nearest bus point to my flat. I repeated the parting message of forgetting everything to the family and thanked them for their free ride.

When i reached my flat it was 8.30 am and with my hypnotised excuses for my overnight stay out, i entered the house to take the hot coffee from my wife.

The news paper carried the warning as i expected.
FINAL WARNING TO VIP CRIMINALS −CONFESS AND SURRENDER WEALTH −OR FACE PUNISHMENT

Under the heading in the front page, a brief summary about −how many criminals who managed to escape punishment from the law till then- why they should be allowed to remain freely without punishment - for the heinous crimes they had committed without protests or opposition and counter attacks from the government, public or from other political parties or social organizations.

In the next paragraph- easy to understand - guidelines were given in simple English to all those who were listed as to what they should do step by step after reading the warning in the paper, within seven days.

The list which was numbered as one- contained 20 names - of top political leaders from the states, including ex-ministers and those who were running political parties in the name of castes, religions and communities. A few leaders were the descendants of those who had participated in the freedom struggle before 1947. A few others who took advantage of the caste and religion started political parties exclusively for people from their own caste /religion. But all of them misused their positions, power and bargained for personal enrichment and did nothing substantial for the people who believed them to be their saviours.

The reading public including the boss of the news paper were not surprised as they were all due for some such punishment for long. But what puzzled the boss was why the editor did not tell him about such a sensational news before publication and what intrigued the team of editors why the boss left the office in a hurry to go to the farm house after giving the material for publication on the next day. When they both finally talked about the matter, both the sides were further confused as the boss could not remember anything about my visit and the same case with the secretaries and the driver. But the supervisor in the farm house was telling his family members that he had a secret to share with them- his boss who was not having any affair with women- till then, had brought someone secretly and stayed with that persons throughout the night. He wanted not any one in the farm house to see the secret person. But he warned his family members that they should not tell anyone. The servants did the same thing but between themselves-in whispers. The boss was not aware of those gossips till now, I suppose.

But the VIPs named and their family members were frozen with fear on seeing the names of their husbands, or fathers, or brothers, or grand-fathers etc in the list. The usual body guards or those who were always remaining close to the leaders, all of them- disappeared leaving their bosses to sort out their problems. The affected families of the listed parties, looked, as if, a cyclone specially formed for them- ravaged only their houses leaving unimaginable disasters everywhere in their households . They were all sitting and not even talking among themselves. Occasionally- one of the members of the family would shout that they should have remained in their own villages minding their own business, when others would shout back to keep their trap shut

Some of the listed persons started acting as per the instructions-immediately after seeing the fate of giants in the political fields for decades having unlimited power of money, political influence and personal killers. A few political anchors who made millions so far were reluctant and wavering but they were strongly advised to comply with the warning or else face punishment from the unknown authority. Except four in the list, from down south in the coastal districts- who felt that they could meet the challenges of the super force- trusting the support of hundreds of muscle men employed by them- others waited till the last day before they surrendered to the nearest police station where all of them confessed to the crimes committed by them – but not all he crimes. They used their discretion and admitted mild to medium strong crimes leaving the murders and rapes completely. Sixteen of the first list did surrender and confess subject to errors and omissions- deliberately done- suppressing the real truth and all the truth

When police read the confession notes of the political and religious criminals, they knew only a small percentage of the total atrocities and crimes had been disclosed withholding carefully many serious crimes – which they had done. But the high command of the police and the government felt that the voluntary disclosure of the criminals were enough to start their investigations and interrogations as per law.

Seven of the listed persons remained in Chennai and three from Madurai – two from Tiruchi and the rest of the eight – two from Virudhunagar, one each from Coimbatore, Salem, Muruganur village- Thondi town - Chengleput and Tirunelveli. The four –two from Tirunelveli and two from Virudhunagar failed to surrender till the last day.

Upon being produced before the magistrate for remanding the alleged criminals for enquiry, the police did not face any problems to get 15 days time for making the preliminary enquiry. Accordingly the seven Chennai city confession- cases were sent to Puzhal jail ;similarly the other nine were jailed in the district HQ jail.

I was watching the progress of the cases from the news papers. After the remanding of the alleged criminals, I had the urge to take up punishment myself without trusting the legal system which might take years with thousands of meaningless hearings. The super power made me to act and I started my preliminary work immediately.

I waited at a distance from the busy police station of Adyar- a prominent locality of Chennai city for an opportunity to get the details I wanted. An hour passed and still there was police officer coming in my direction. Suddenly I remembered the name of the SI at the ex-CM 's house but I had no chance to bring him to the place I wanted. While I was engrossed in my thoughts – I saw a police car coming out from the station- might be an Asst. commissioner. I plunged into action not willing to leave the chance when it came on its own. I waved the car to stop. The police driver was taken aback- a civilian on the road had the guts to stop the car of a police officer- he stopped the vehicle as if he was about to hit me. He looked at me and that was all he knew. He smiled at me. The officer who was seated on the backseats of the car- a senior policeman- looking with authority and arrogance written all over his face turned his attention me. I took a few seconds and he also came under control. I opened the door and got inside it without waiting for permission or invitation.

I asked the driver to go cruising as I had to talk to his boss. Quickly I asked him about the procedure for police interrogation in the case of the seven criminals who had confessed- where they would be kept-over night –when they would be interrogated- who would do it. How to go to the spot of the interrogation and who was the final authority for those cases under police enquiry etc. He replied to all my questions as he happened to a senior asst commissioner marked for promotion to deputy commissioner within three months. He appeared to me as a strict officer and I thanked him and told him and the driver -my usual parting instructions and got down in a place which was deserted.

I walked further in the opposite direction and boarded a bus that was about to leave. I took a ticket for a place known to me in the city which was on the way to the destination and after getting down from the bus- took an auto to my place- mesmerizing the driver just as a measure of abundant precaution and alighted from it a kilometer away from my flat. I paid the driver and asked him to forget etc and once the auto left in the direction of the city. I legged the distance to my flat.

On the next day after noon around 3 pm, I left my house on some concocted pretext- reached the office of a particular IG - law and order and police enquiry. I could not make a daring entry under the eyes of many police men on duty. I had to do it under discretion. With the personal mobile number of the IG -given to me by the AC on the previous day- I contacted him and asked him to meet me at a place I selected near his office to tell him about the identity of the unknown force which had been killing VVIPs recently. But I warned him not to do any police tricks and come alone to get the information and leave.

I waited for him to act as per instructions. I was told by the AC that the IG was a clean man without any black marks and he was a dare-devil and had unearthed several cases of serious crimes throughout his illustrious career. I saw a police car coming slowly and someone from it was scanning both the sides. I knew that it was the IG and I waved at the car from where I was standing behind a parked lorry. He came near me and looked at me. I controlled his mind on the spot and got into the car immediately.

I told him to go to the police HQ where the seven criminals confessed recently and he did without any reaction. I heaved a sigh or else what would happen to me- I dreaded to think. The drive took us an hour in the heavy traffic and once he entered the HQ- there were salutes after salutes and he straight drove to the place where the police enquires were conducted. Being the in-charge of the department- his presence electrified the police men present. I took out the black purdha which I purchased from Triplicane Muslim cloth store- on my way back to the flat the day before and wore it like a muslim lady and got down with the IG. I told him to take me to the enquiry spot where the seven criminals were being questioned. Normally only one at a time would be brought from the central jail for interrogation and the seven alleged criminals being ex-VIPs already confessed to the crimes themselves, the police officials thought it better to bring all of them together to avoid any untoward incidents on the way as major part of their was made easy by the self-declaration of the crimes by the VIPs.

On seeing their boss coming with a Muslim lady with a body veil- all the police men and officers were surprise. Bu they thought that the most intelligent officer of the Tamil nadu knew better to bring a Muslim lady to the HQ and there should be a strong reason for his action. They started minding their work. I accompanied the top ranking officer through a maze of lanes inside the building and finally reached a big hall where the enquiry was going on. One of the seven was seated and the police interrogator was busy in getting the information he wanted from the criminal. But when he saw the IG he stopped and saluted him.

I told the IG to send all the policemen from the hall forthwith which he did. We were two on the scene and I asked the IG to close the door and bolt it inside. He did.
I removed the purdha and took out the blank papers with a ball pen and gave it to the VIP leader after bringing him under my control –to write down all the crimes he had committed till then. The criminal started immediately as if he was waiting for such an assignment. I asked the IG to tell the officer in charge to bring the rest of the VIP criminal- over the mobile phone. Within five minutes i heard the tapping of the door to hall from outside. I asked the IG to open it while I remained behind the door opened inwardly. The six culprits entered one by one and once they were inside, I told the IG to close the door and bolt it inside.

The six notorious characters looked at me and were brought under my control then and there. Thereafter I told them to sit down and gave them each a bunch of blank papers with ball pen and told them to write down everything they had done unlawfully or illegally till then. All the seven were busy like writing an examination and it took nearly one hour and fifity minutes for all the seven to complete their confessions. I asked the IG to go to sleep when the seven were busy with the work given to them.

Once all of them had finished, I woke up the IG and told him to call the officer in charge in side. He did. Within a few minutes, the door was opened for him to enter and when he saw me, I hypnotized him also.

I then asked all the seven to go and stand in a row facing the wall. They obeyed my orders quickly. I asked all the seven criminals to repeat after me – " we have committed grave crimes. We deserve death sentence only. We want to be shot dead. Our death should open the eyes of those who have plans to loot the country in the name of politics. Those who are being listed should confess to all the crimes and irregularities- without trying to withhold the truth or else they would also face this treatment only. It is better to get the punishment by the law than face the bullets like us. Long live Tamil nadu Long live India"

I then handed over the revolver with silencer which I brought from Mumbai guards and gave it to the IG..He was looking over the heavy gun in his hands when I asked all the seven to turn around and face us. They did .

I asked the IG to shoot the first four of the criminals through their chests. He did and the silencer muffled the noise of the gun firing but still the room reverberated with the gun shots. Once he had completed the job given to him, I gave another silencer gun to the inspector and asked him to shoot the remaining three through their chests. He did what he was told. The seven once very important persons in the society had become very much dead bodies.

I took both the revolvers from them- which I could use later- and packed them in the bag I brought with me- hidden by the veil. I then told the inspector to come with me and the IG . I told him to give strict instructions to other police men who were waiting outside the enquiry hall- not to open the hall door till he returned back to the spot after some time. He went out and came back after doing what I have asked him to do.

I then asked the IG to leave. I with veil over my body and the two police officers acting like my body guards -till we reached the official car of the IG . I opened the car door and got into the car first followed by the IG while I asked the inspector to drive the car out of the HQ.

Once we were on the public roads, I asked the inspector to take us to the central station. I asked the inspector to stop the vehicle just a few metres away from the bus stand opposite to the central station. When he did, I told both the officers to forget etc and removed my purdha. Safely keeping it in the bag- I got down on the right side of the car- where the vehicles were crossing the parked car fast. I used the kerchief trick and asked the inspector to go to the HQ. I still covering my face with the kerchief reached the mainstream of passengers moving towards the platform of the busiest station. I mixed with the crowd. With a platform ticket I went inside the biggest station of Southern Railway and took a strong doze of hot coffee. Through another entrance to the station I came out of the station and took an auto . I mesmerized him immediately and asked to go to a busy place on my way to my house. Once I reached the intermediary halt, I paid the auto driver and told him the usual advice to forget everything and leave. Once he had gone, I took the next bus to my place and got down at the nearest bus stand to my flat.

When I reached the house, it was nearing ten in the night. With the usual excuses under mantra effect I managed that day and after dinner- slept peacefully by applying the mantra effect on me.

The IG's shoot out in the jail created a storm in the police HQs while the media capitalized it as usual. Nobody could digest the fact how a senior most IG could shoot the prisoners under police custody for enquires. Even the concerned IG could not believe and the same case with the dozens of police constables and the inspector of the enquiry team. The High court had condemned the shooting and ordered for the arrest of the IG and the team- suo motto. . The CM was shell-shocked and hurriedly sent an emissary with a detailed report to the home ministry of the government of India to confirm that the law and order situation was intact in the state, fearing promulgation of President rule under article 356.

The bodies of the seven were handed over to the relatives who did not raise hue and cry which they would have done under normal Indian democratic circumstances which was prevailing before the emergency of the unknown person and his or her brutal punishments of the escapees of crimes for decades.

On the third day after the shootout in the jail, I prepared the next list of the second batch of ex-ministers containing the news of 43 corrupt persons- but misused their positions and committed innumerable offences under the law. I put it along with the copies of the confessions of the seven who were shot dead- in a thick-cloth cover. After sealing it neatly, I addressed it to the Publisher of the news paper in bold letters with many warnings that it should be opened by him only . I then went to the nearest place to the office of the English daily. I waited for sometime before picking up the right person for doing the job- a college student. I brought him under my control and gave the cover containing the list to him asking him to go the front office of the news paper and give it to the person in charge telling that the cover contained an important message for the publisher and editor. I asked him that he should meet me at the same place after delivering the cover.

The student did what I told him as I was watching him at a distance. I saw that no one was following him and when he came to me as per instructions, I told him the parting instructions to be followed and walked into an small street leading to the busiest electronic market of the state. I got drowned in the crowd and through the opposite street, I came out to the busy main road and took a bus to an intermediary place on the way to my house.

The next day- the English daily carried the Xerox copies of the confessions of the seven persons- except the details of the hideouts of the cash and properties which were withheld and not included in press release by me purposely as I wanted to think it over about its good use for the public welfare. From the beginning of the mission of punishments- I did not want the political administration to go after the ill-gotten wealth which they also would not use properly. The net result was devastating- people reacted violently demanding the arrest of others involved in the irregularities and criminal activities of the seven-specifically named by them before being shot. The media did their best to spread the message that no longer politics was an easy means to make money or commit crimes. The police did their best to arrest all those named in the confession notes and the CM immediately conducted a top level cabinet meeting to declare their assets earned by them in normal course.

The four remaining in the list surrendered to the nearest police station where they had given an unabridged confession note giving minute details of all the crimes and irregularities they had committed naming those who were involved in all the criminal activities. Others remanded to police custody in the district HQ jails -came out clean on seeing the fate of the seven and wrote their second detailed confession notes without suppressing the whole truth.

The 43 persons named – most of them ex-ministers- surrendered to the nearest police HQ of the district as I had given them only 48 hours -to surrender and confess. I also told them in the message that they should mention the names of the corrupt officials who were helping them, the persons who committed the crimes on their behalf and others who were benefitted by their misuse of power- including the businessmen.

The effect was tremendous and the medias were full with the news about the 43 persons and the staggering list of crimes they had committed with the names of those where accomplices to their misdeeds. The police force of Tamilnadu was overworking for the first time after fifty years with hundreds of arrests, filing of cases, producing the alleged criminals to the courts for getting permission to conduct the police enquiry and in short, there was a violent storm-like situation in the minds of certain sections of the people while outwardly the medias projected an unusual happiness and relief among the major voting public. The interviews with the public right from a remote village deep in the southern part of the state to the high class educated and business persons revealed an uniform satisfaction and gratitude to the unknown person who had put a full stop to the gross misuse of the democratic political powers for enriching the politicians from the day one of the independence to the country.

But the work which was started by the mantra effect appeared to be a long drawn process. Te first two lists only contained 63 prominent persons- but go beyond them was not possible for me unless I got some help. I thought about the avenues open to me for getting the details for the next lists. To go to police department was not advisable as they would first arrest me before thinking about the larger welfare of the public- because- many of the top officials of the police over the past several decades were involved in several irregularities and misuse of powers for personal benefit like the politicians.

Hence my choice finally fell on the magazines reporting crimes and other unlawful and illegal activities not only in the politics but in every phase of the society I chose one such crime reporting magazine known for authenticated unbiased cases . On a fine morning after morning food- that was my practice for years- I went to the main business road- Anna salai of Chennai- and got down near the office of the print media. I walked casually and reached the security kiosk . An elderly security man peeped through an opening from the kiosk and asked me what I wanted.

I took him in my control and he allowed me freely inside. At the reception desk- a cute little thing around 25 sat with mobile on her ear and was spreading her charm around. When she saw me –she disconnected the phone and with a trade mark smile asked how she could help me. I brought her 98under my spell. She accompanied me to the cabin of the chief editor –not only that- she knocked the door and went inside with me tagging along- and introduced me to the boss who was in a meeting with some of the staff.

There was a look of anger mixed confusion on the face of the boss who looked at me and I had to cut short lot of unwanted wastage of time to complete my work of gathering the details I was after. He instantly stood up to shake hands with me- but there were people in front of him- he told them to come later and asked me sit down. The reception bird and the staff departed immediately leaving me with the well-known person in the Tamilnadu press club.

I quickly told what I wanted.- the names of all the MLAs, MPs who had won -from the first elections to the last one- the names of all the private educational engineering-medical and arts colleges, deemed universities- the names of all the illicit liquor barons –the names of top ranking real estate giants- the names of government officials who had been reported to have given patta for house sites – on the lakes around the cities, towns, and villages- on the public lands- the names of corrupt police officials irrespective of their ranks- the names of all IAS and other services officers who were corrupt till their retirement and who were still in service- the names of registering authorities of vehicles, properties from the beginning till that date- the names of PWD officials who made millions by bribes and the list of approved government contractors and the list of improper completion of the public projects- and the resultant loss of public funds and loss of lives of innocent beneficiaries.

He was listening to me with open eyes and for the first time, I wanted a person other than me to know about the mission I was asked to undertake by some unknown power. I released him from the mantra effect. He took time to come around and the first thing he wanted to know- who I was. I then told him

I then told him briefly about me without bringing in the mantra backup- and frankly admitted my involvement in the punishment of the VVIPs including the corrupt CM and his families. I detected an abject fear on his face and he was sweating profusely . I asked him to clean his face and continued my confession to the extent to which it was desirable.

He was looking aghast and remained silent without reacting. Then I gave the lists of names I wanted. He went through them and asked for the first time opening his mouth-

"Sir, are you going to punish these people like those you have already listed?"

I said that was the general idea. He wiped his face once again and did know what to do and say.

I asked him-" Mr Editor- don't you want these bad elements punished ? All these years you only reported thousands of cases of how criminals got away without punishment. You only wanted someone should come and stop these people from carrying on their nefarious activities without fear of punishment. Is it not?"

He stared at me and when I asked him to reply- he nodded his head.

" Then please give the information one by one. When you are ready with the names of the first category of criminals – please indicate you readiness in your weekly twice- magazine indirectly at some page only for me to understand. I will come and collect it .You know that if I want- I can do anything to get my mission completed. Why in your case, I came out openly because- you are going to be the leader of the mission from now on. You give the list and I will publish the names in the English daily- the culprits surrender and confess. Once all the listed persons do what I expect them to do, i will contact you from a public phone to inform me about the status of the next list and so on- till I exhaust the names of all those criminals who should be behind the bars. I have a master plan for using the ill-gotten wealth of all those I have punished and am going to use it for the public welfare. I will discuss with you later. Now, are you willing to join the mission or not – please tell me openly now?"

He appeared to be in a trance without my mantra effect. All along he was editing the true stories of unlawful and illegal activities of political and other types of criminal. But when the question of taking the role of taking action against the bad elements arose, he was hesitating. All these guys I felt were all paper tigers .

" Hello- are you alright?" I had to remind him when he shrugged himself and said-

" How can I join your mission? Only police can help you. But on my part, I can give the names list by list- but beyond that- I do not want to be a party to your actions- taking law in your hands and punishing people including killing them brutally. " he was not a paper tiger- a bold paper tiger at that.

I appreciated his frankness and told him or rather warned him- " look my dear friend- I offered the leader post only based on your years of yearning for cleaning the society and punishing the anti-social elements. I have found that you are a chicken-hearted paper tiger. Ok. Persons like you are undesirable companions for noble missions. It is a war I am waging against the corruption and anti-public activities. You are well known editor of a crime reporting magazine. I find that you are fit for reporting and nothing more. Fine. Now listen to me- I want the lists one by one- you shall not tell anyone meeting me or talking to me- or about my offer or about the list. Under some pretext you shall get the lists from your office. If you think you are smart and do something to reveal my identity or tell the English daily about me or to the police or to your friends, or your family or any one- you have seen the photos of the ex-CM the great founder of the main opposition party today when he was punished by me- that would be nothing before the punishment which I would give to you and to your family members- It is a promise. Now get started without further discussion as I am fed up with your cowardice and fake interests in public welfare" I did not spit on his face but face did it.

He bowed down his head and did not have guts to raise it to see me straight.

I demanded a promise from him before I left the place. He simply said " Sorry sir, but the lists will be made available. I will never think of disclosing your identity. I will follow your instructions correctly. I promise"

I stood up and he looked at me. I hypnotized him and asked him to go to sleep. I did not tell him to forget anything about our meeting. I had taken a risk but let me see- what he did. I knew that always I could enter the scene and set right the mistakes if any in the process of getting the lists I wanted .

I came out to the reception and the receptionist free from my matra effect was surprised to look at me. I had to bring her under my control as I wanted her to forget my visit till she saw me leaving the office. I repeated the same thing with the security person and once out on the main road, mission completed, I crossed the road through the underground subway. I took an auto back home and after the usual instructions to the auto driver I walked down the last kilo metre to reach my flat to tell my wife the usual cock and bull story for my outing.

The next week was an uneventful one –only for me and for the general public- it was a week of thrilling actions of police arresting those who were involved in the crimes of the VVIPs listed for surrender and confession.

I was going through the Tamil weekly twice issue of the crime reporting magazine. After three issues, there was a meaningless message in one of the pages-

" Listed -M-LAMP; get free- "

I got the message which was meant for me. I went to the nearest point to the office of the magazine and stopped an unaccompanied a beautiful young woman, on her way to some place busily. I mesmerized her and told her to meet the editor and bring a closed cover he would give to her. She did what I told her. I gave her a small memo paper wherein I asked her to write –listed M-LAMP get free- paper tiger" I told her to show it to the editor only and tell the security that only the editor wanted her to come and see him. I contacted him over the public phone and told him that I would come to collect the list at any time on that day with a warning not to do anything smart.

She went and after twenty minutes came back and gave the thick closed cover. I told her to forget everything and asked her to proceed in the direction towards which she was walking when I stopped her.

Once at home, I prepared the next list of all the ex-MPs first who were elected from the first election and who were reported to be corrupt and have made enormous wealth by misuse of powers etc. I had specifically told the editor that only bad elements must be included in his list leaving the good ones.

On the next day I got the list delivered to the English daily publisher and he dutifully published it with the usual messages of warning and the procedure to be followed. The media entertainment continued for the public who were waiting for the next list as per first message. They were happy visibly on seeing the names of those whose atrocities with the power of the member of parliament knew no bounds and who were moving around in the country as VIPs getting undeserving concessions and privileges.

The time given to them was just 48 hours only and I added that those who did not respond within the time limit would be facing the bullet treatment even if there was a delay of one day. That did the trick- all the 355 corrupt MPs out of the 480 and odd total Tamil nadu MPs elected so far in the sixteen general elections- and bye elections- surrendered and submitted the detailed list of irregularities committed by them- alone- with others help without suppressing the facts to the extent to which they could remember.

The cases were registered along with hundreds of similar cases already under police and judicial scrutiny. The medias blown out of proportion - the role of the unknown power without which it would not have been possible to bring all the corrupt politicians under books just like that with a news paper warning .

The MPs list was followed by the MLA list- but I got it published it in a lot of four districts of the state at a time as there were 4122 MLAs elected so far in the elections conducted so far in the state. The response was as expected. The corrupt and unruly MLAs surrendered and subjected themselves to the crime and punishment system of the government.

But the biggest question remained unanswered in the minds of the people, police and government- because I did not ask the culprits to disclose the same in their confessions. What happened to the ill-gotten wealth of the political criminals so far? I had to think about it only after I exhaust the lists of the criminals of the state of Tamilnadu. It would take another one or two months depending upon the speed with which the crime reporting magazine office staff culled out the details called for by me.

I checked up the lists I wanted from the editor of the Tamil magazine to find out where the mission stood vis-à-vis the lists given.

the names of all the MLAs, MPs who had won -from the first elections to the last one- OVER

That was all. I had to get the remaining 10 lists to bring all those who made democracy meaningless ever since the country became independent. If people had waited 64 years, there was nothing wrong, if my mission took another few months to remove the undesirable characters from the public circulation .I told myself-

That it took not three months- but six months and to be exact six months and twenty three days to get the last report.
the names of all the private educational engineering-medical and arts colleges, Deemed universities-
the names of all the illicit liquor barons –
the names of top ranking real estate giants-
the names of government officials who had been reported to have given patta for house sites – on the lakes around the cities, towns, and villages- on the public lands-
the names of corrupt police officials irrespective of their ranks-

113

the names of all IAS and other services officers who were corrupt till their retirement and who were still in service-
the names of registering authorities of vehicles, properties from the beginning till that date-
the names of PWD officials who made millions by bribes and
the list of approved government contractors and
the list of improper completion of the public projects- and the resultant loss of public funds and loss of lives of innocent beneficiaries.

The courts were full with the thousands of cases relating to the confessed crimes by the politicians and others who were enjoying a carefree criminal life. I sent a warning to the judges- lawyers and the government through the English daily that the cases should be disposed off within three months from the date of filing - as there was nothing for the police or the courts - to do their usual time consuming work. I demanded the government to set up sufficient special courts and use the retired judges and also to increase the number of judges in the existing courts. I wanted that the cases should be heard and finalized by any court-in the state- from the Municif and district courts to the High courts and the special courts at each district HQ. My warning ended up with an exclusive punishment to the Chief Minister and the concerned department secretary and top officials if there was a delay in establishing the special courts or increasing the strength of the judges.

The result- within nine months- Tamilnadu became the only state in the entire Independent India to have punished all the politicians and other types of criminals misusing the public funds and welfare schemes.

Sorry for the break-

The readers should know how I did ensure 100 % true confession from the thousands of criminals within nine months – simple. From every list I picked up at random a few cases of fairly well known persons from the city and the district HQ and personally attended the hearings. At the courts as usual normally picked up the close relatives like son, daughter or wife or friend etc and through them I made the accused to confess once again in the courts. If the court found that the confession already by that accused at the police station at the time of surrender remained almost the same, I wound leave the court hall without harming the accused. But if I found that there was large scale suppression of facts or truths or telling of lies , through the relatives of the accused- I would punish the accused in the court- death sentence with bullet shots in the chest at close range. Normally I had to mesmerize the police officer carrying service revolver – accompanying the VIP and relieve the gun from him once I found that the accused had to be punished by me and not by the court. Once the accused was shot I would retreat from the scene quietly . Thus I established firmly in the minds of the thousands of criminals who confessed that they would

114

be shot dead if they had not confessed fully or included lies. There were many revised confessions before the hearing and in the process- seventy four accused were punished by me when I went for test checking to the courts- right from the beginning.

Now to continue from where I have left-

The work done by the editor and the staff of the magazine was commendable.

I have decided to meet the editor personally and accordingly left my house at 11 am the right time for meeting any top bosses. I took a bus to the office and at the security gate, I changed my strategy without using the mantra. I told him that the editor only wanted me to come and see him that day. Without any hesitation he waved me inside and at the reception, I repeated the same thing to a new male receptionist but I added that he should tell the editor that a paper tiger had come to see him. He contacted the editor and told him exactly what I told him. I was asked to proceed to the first floor office of the editor.

I knocked the door and entered the spacious –but full of books and documents etc. The editor a popular writer stood up to greet me and said –

" I am indeed honored by your visit. Please tell me what else I should do now? "

I did not use my mantra effect even at that stage. I knew that I could use it anytime when the goings were becoming disadvantageous to my anonymous entity . I smiled back and took the seat offered.

" I have come here personally to thank you and your staff for completing the mission successfully. But I cannot meet all your staff personally as I want to remain as an unidentified force till the remaining part of my mission is over. Please convey my thanks to them" while extending my hand to thank him at least.

Presently the door was opened and a spate of office staff entered – all of them greeting me in chorus and I stood up taken by surprise while the editor was in all smiles introducing them as those who helped him to get the details I wanted from him.

Even at that stage I did not feel like mesmerizing them. But the unexpected happened –mobile cameras- regular cameras flashed. I was photographed. I felt that it would ruin my image as a unknown force and hence I wanted to seize the cameras and mobiles. I used the mantra effect on all of them strongly.

But to my horror, there was no visible change on any one. They continued to thank me and my one-man war with the criminals and the corrupt persons of the state. They were saying many things but I was standing there grinning- like a head of the family caught red-handed stealing the cookies at midnight by other members of the family- foolishly but those present were not worried whether I was happy or shocked. But the fact remained that the unknown force was nothing but an old man with grey hair- it would become public soon and I would be a sitting duck to kill- for the innumerable persons who were directly or indirectly affected by my mission over the past one year.

I felt that the curtains were lifted and I have become a public entity and I should be ready to face the consequences . It took some time for me get back my normal spirit. I thanked them all shaking hands with them while being photographed. I was offered a flower bouquet- a shawl – the usual Tamilnadu style of honoring guests of honor. I accepted them and bidding goodbye not only to them but to the 'unknown status' which made it possible for me to take up and complete the mission. The entire team with the editor came out to give me a send off despite my protest. When I told them that I would return to my place by bus – they were shocked. Immediately the editor called the driver of his car and told him to bring the vehicle forthwith. The entire staff and the editor literally pushed me inside the car with the driver to drop me at my residence safely. They were happily waving their hands till the car took a turn to the main road.

I asked the driver to stop on the Old Mahapalipuram road – near a junction and told him that my house was inside a lane where the car could not go and without waiting for his reply I walked quickly in the nearest lane – leaving the flower bouquet and the shawl on the floor of the car. I did not want them with me as it would be embarrassing to take them in the bus. I did not want an auto as the mantra effect had gone.

At the flat, I did not lie and told my wife everything from the time I realized that the mantra effect gave me the power to make people do what I wanted them to do- from the incident one to the latest visit of thanksgiving to the staff and the editor of the magazine. She sat like a wax statute and from her eyes I could detect only the fear of punishment for me for all the crimes I had committed while carrying out the mission with mantra effect. I did not expect anything better from an orthodox Brahmin housewife-because I would have reacted exactly in the same way like my wife.

She started crying and I left her to feel for my actions as I did not know how I could console her. I myself was worried about what would happen to me ever since-I became publically known in the presence of the staff of the magazine.

116

I was in my room and my wife was in hers, when the TV blared with the flash news-

"secret of unknown force   made known-" punch line of one TV channel.

"at last – the person behind the war against criminals- is an old man" another TV channel

" an old man –behind the success story of eradication of criminals in Tamilnadu"

The TV showed my photos from different angles- taken by the staff of the magazine and to top it, my stay at the magazine office till I was a given a send off was telecasted. The TV channels got the views of general public and government officials. When the public response was in favor of me and my mission, the officials and a few of the well-known persons in the society were very cautious while appreciating me and at the same time did not approve my method of punishing the criminals. They felt that the criminals should have been handed over to the police from the beginning and not after staging barbarous way of punishing the guilty with acid and bullets.

There were mixed response- for my mission- but the majority was in favour of giving me the highest civilian honour like Nobel prize - Bharat Rathna or Paramarveer chakra - and there were sections of people- who demanded a trial for me for the crimes committed while punishing the criminals or else they argued that others also would follow me and take the law in their hands to punish crimes as they liked. The police chief told that the matter was under active consideration as to what should be done after knowing the identity of the unknown person and they would come out with their action plan soon. The chief minister was evasive and did not reply to the question about the action against me –whether it would be against or in favour of me.

In the meantime, those who were affected and whose family members were punished by the courts did not remain quiet. They started coming out openly demanding my arrest and action against me for what I had done in the name of punishing the criminals. The Central government also was in a fix because they had to answer the spate of questions from the human rights commission and other well known social workers demanding a fair enquiry against me though they appreciated what I had done. But their contention was that I had transgressed the boundaries of law and order of the country and acted like Robin hood in 2011.

The matter was the most discussed issue not only in our country and other countries as well. The pressure mounted day by day from Prime Ministers and Presidents of other countries and the chief ministers and other political leaders of other states.

The axe fell on one fine morning when the police who traced me easily. They announced a cash award for anyone to come forward to identify me. Several persons known to me from the places I stayed till then and others who knew me well went rushing to identify me. The police chief personally came to arrest me- but all politeness, he asked me to come with him and he assured my wife and other family members who were with me ever since my identity was made known public- that I would given the due respect as a freedom fighter or a military general and not like a criminal. They were shedding tears when I was taken out ceremoniously to the waiting personal car of the DGP. I told my family members that there should be no bail application drama and I was ready to face the charges single handedly as I carried out the mission alone.

On the way, the police boss was kind enough to tell me to bear with him and others and he saw me only as a divine avatar and not like a killer. I thanked him. At the police HQ, I was given a separate room with cot, fan, and bed sheets pillow and an attached bath. The DGP and other top officials visited me one after other. They shook hands with me strangely and assured me that I would be treated with all honours and my arrest was to satisfy the demand for trial for me by a section of the people- the relatives and friends of the criminals and also to satisfy the human rights commission.

I slept that night peacefully. On the next day after 11 am I was produced before a magistrate at Egmore where I was asked whether I would like to deny or admit my crimes. I said proudly that I would like to plead guilty for all the crimes I had committed. The magistrate did not know what to do. He asked the police officials to take me back to prison till the hearing started as per legal process. But the police officials took be to an isolated place at the back of the HQ of police and there I was asked to stay till the court took up the case. I found the new place more convenient and comfortable- except the presence of my family members. One of the guards explained to me that I could not be sent to any jail because all those criminals confessed and sentenced were there in all most all the jails in the state – some of them waiting to be hanged till death. Hence, the CM told the police that I should be given top grade protection as there were many who would be waiting for an opportunity to take revenge against me.

Further already reports have started coming about the whereabouts of the wealth and cash belonging to those who were punished by me including those seven at the police HQ. The relatives and friends of the punished had reported the missing movable assets of the family members and they were suspecting that I had kept them secretly somewhere. But the main agitation was for my arrest only and perhaps after they achieved their first demand- they might demand to know where I had kept the assets of the criminals.

I plainly told the innumerable media persons that I had nothing to hide . I told them that I was proud to have completed my mission of eradicating the criminals ruling the state knowing that the present laws did not approve of my methods. I was cheerfully when I said that I was ready to sacrifice my life for the noble cause. They shouted back to me that they would not allow the government to punish a good Samaritan like me −"come what may"- they also shook hands with me.

On the second day of my arrest, the DGP and the Commissioner of Police came to see me. They did not allow anyone else to remain the hall. After the few formal enquiries they brought the case of the IG who shot the seven alleged criminals under custodial enquiry . I told them that my mission was to eliminate the seven treacherous gangsters and perhaps I had done injustice to the honest and brave officer in the larger interest of the mission. Actually if the IG wanted to punish me, I would tell the court that he was not responsible for his action and he was mesmerized by me to commit the crimes. They were surprised to hear me speak so frankly and said that they would get back to me after discussing with the IG in prison.

On the third day after my arrest, when I was reading the news papers and magazines, when a top police officer entered the hall where I was kept with police guards on all sides- and saluted me first. He then told me that the Chief minister would be seeing me that day at 4 pm. I said that it was a honour done to a criminal like me but he smiled back and said- " not a criminal-sir".

He left me with a salute .

At 4 pm-sharp to the minute, there was a shuffle and noise outside my room and within a few minutes, police guards appeared followed by a white and white dressed person- the Chief Minister with his normal entourage. I stood up as a chair was brought for the CM to sit comfortably. He made some signal and immediately no one remained in the big hall except me and the CM.

Once he was sure that no one was present- he stood up and came towards me- and when I was not expecting the least- he prostrated before me saying that I was a saint or divine personality- or else no one could have done what I had done. I lifted him and asked him to take his seat. I was so nervous by the sudden gesture of the CM of a state- who must be thinking that I still possessed some extra-ordinary powers. The political big wigs always blindly believed some god men and acted as per their advice only. This CM perhaps was thinking of making his Raj Guru or something for his safe journey till the end of his tenure or he was indirectly thanking me for having spared him despite his own quota of crimes. I did not bother as I did not have the power any more.

He told me that it was he who instructed the police to keep me in that place and to see that I was not disturbed or harmed by anyone. I thanked him. He said that the law would take its course but no harm would come to me as no one was interested to punish a person who freed the state from rowdies, corrupt officials and political criminals- excluding him of course. I did not say a word in reply. I listened to him patiently. He finally requested me to leave everything to him and he would use all his powers to see that I came out unscathed. He had already met some senior authorities of judiciary who he said were not interested in proceeding against me legally for the yeomen service done to the people of the state. He left after twenty minutes with the folded hands and almost tears on his eyes. Before he was about to leave- I told him to make use of the assets seized from the list of criminals for the public welfare to the last rupee with a request that no irregularity should be allowed in any form. He came back to assure that he had already learnt from me and that during his rest of his term he would work only for the welfare of the people without misusing powers for his personal enrichment. I thanked him and told him that I had some plans which I would discuss with him later. He bowed and tapped the door of the hall. The police officers and other government officials were waiting for him outside and with them he went to the waiting car.

I sat for some time just to get out of the after effect of the CM's visit – particularly the act of falling down at my feet.

The first hearing was posted within two weeks after my arrest as the case was given top priority by the high court. There were no charge sheets normally to be given to the alleged criminal and in my case, I openly admitted to all the crimes attributed to unknown force in front of police officials, magistrate and the media people. The case sheets were already there and I refused to take them telling that they could go ahead and charge me as per the law.

But I felt that some force was behind the quickening of the case so that I need not have to be there in that lonely place too long. Anyway- the usual procedural delay in similar cases to mine would have taken a year or so with innumerable applications for bail etc or finding fault in the charge sheet or demanding details and plethora of reasons available with the lawyers for adjournment on cases of mega frauds or political crimes.

Just before the first hearing, I met my wife, sons and daughter in laws who were trying to see me many times before –which I did not allow because I did not want them to come here and cry. I knew they would come to the court and make a scene. Hence I called them and told them squarely that some unknown force which still remained somewhere and which empowered me with the mantra knew- what it should do in my case. Hence they should not come to the court and create scene there. But they pleaded vehemently and wife started weeping. I had to agree to her request but I got her promise not to embarrass me in the court.

The hearing was scheduled at 10.30 in the No 2 court which was the biggest one in the High court. The case was handled by a full bench including the chief justice besides four other senior judges. The state versus me was the most talked about news in the state, national and even in the international medias. There was a posse of one thousand police men, excluding the riot police, water gun truck etc just to prevent any calamity or law and order problem from the families and friends- cadres from political parties whose leaders were punished because of me.

I was taken with heaviest security which no one was given in the recent history to the court and there in the court, I was surrounded by a number of policemen with AK -47 ready in their hands. When the judges came one by one I paid my respects to them with my folded hands. But what shocked me was their return gesture of showing me respect with their folded hands.

I stood there facing the Advocate general specially named for my case and he was assisted by a dozen government senior public prosecutors. The GDP and the commissioner of police were seated with them. They smiled at me with respect.

The case was announced by the court staff. Thereafter the Chief Justice asked the Advocate general to start his case.

He bowed before the judges and said-

"in my career as a government pleader to the present post- I have seen thousands of cases and out of them now and then there were some peculiar cases were brought to the courts. But this is the first time"- he stopped for a second before looking at me- " a court is brought before the court- I mean- an individual who acted as a super court in awarding punishment to those who managed to escape punishment for their heinous crimes from the legal courts of this nation for years. Though the action taken by the person was violation of law but I am forced to admit that without the violation and with the set of laws we have with us – there was not even a remotest chance to punish those who were curses to the state-masquerading as politicians, government officials, government contractors, underground dadas or mafias, educationists, arrack shop magnets. That this great person took the law in his hands- was definitely illegal and wrong – every Indian leave alone the Tamilian knew – but was there any alternative for taking actions against the category of criminals I just now listed? Either the people of this state should have continued to tolerate the anti-public activities of those criminals and their family members or should raise up collectively to punish them.

Would that work out- just think? Who would be the fittest person to lead such public agitations- like the French revolution ? There would be hundreds of meetings and millions of discussions. Who would be ready to fight against the known criminals and their muscle men or bodyguards and the party cadres- the gangsters- rowdies- paid killers- illicit arrack merchants- pimps and smugglers? Which civilian has the training and expertise to fight with these ruffians and dangerous thugs? Therefore even if all the people agree and are ready to take action- there is no way they could organize and lead their attacks against the highly organized criminal networks. Hence, I conclude that this unselfish good Samaritan standing there humbly had done what every one of the sixty millions Tamilians wanted to do themselves –of course- only in their dreams. But I am surprised to see this youngest old man took it upon himself -with missionary spirit to completely free this state from VIP criminals - as an one man army. Your honour, what I have said till now , were the views of the advocate general of the state as a person and not as the government official.

Now, as the leader of the team of prosecutors of the government- I have to tell frankly that we have no evidence of any kind to implicate this person standing there as the accused except his own admission to the crimes. We have no finger prints- foot prints- eye witnesses- incriminatory documents- or telephonic talks of conspiring with his accomplices- no complaints against him personally by any of the affected persons- till now. Only on his own admission, the world had come to know that he was the unknown force who was punishing the free lance criminals- and neither the police nor other agencies of the government, on their own -found out who the unknown force was. Even now I do not know whether the person standing in the defendant box is the real unknown force or he is trying to divert our attention and hampering our investigations to trace the real unknown force. In view of the fact that our charges are based only on the voluntary admissions of the defendant in this case, the prosecution prays to the honourable court to permit us to proceed with the case on the self declaration of the accused only."

He bowed and returned to his seat. There was utter silence in the biggest court hall. No one even whispered. I was terribly impressed by the speech of the advocate general. I looked at him with admiration.

The Judges were discussing with themselves for some time. The chief justice said that the case was adjourned for considering the technicality of the appeal of the prosecution and it would be taken up on the next day. They rose up and smiling at me they left the court to their chambers one by one.

The police security immediately took me by hand and safely conducted me to the waiting police van and within a few minutes I was on my way to the place where I was kept neither like a prisoner nor like a free man.

The next day the court precincts were jam packed with top police officers-the media persons, local, national and international press reporters, policemen wielding riot control tools besides, top lawyers of the country, CM's emissary, and my family members. Many were struggling to get a foothold in the court hall.
I was brought like a invaluable treasure with commandos on all sides to the defendant box of the court hall. When i entered the all all those who were there before me stood up with folded hands and i reciprocated their greetings. Within the next few minutes the judges came one by one and after greeting me with their smiles sat down. The chief justice asked the special prosecutor for the case to start on the basis of his request on the previous day. The AG bowed before the judges and thanked him.
Before he could start his case, four leading lawyers of the nation stood up and asked the court's permission to represent the defendant who refused to have any lawyer to represent him on the previous day.
(already sent by email)
The Chief justice before taking decision asked me whether i had changed my mind on the issue of a lawyer for me. I said that i was a retired bank officer –living on my pension and my sons support –I could not even imagine to engage lawyers leave alone the giants who wanted to appear for me. I turned towards the lawyers and thanked them while i flatly told them that i could not afford them besides my case was an open and shut case.

The four lawyers bowed their heads before me and said that they had come on their own and there was no question of fees for the case. It was the duty of every law knowing Indian to come to my rescue and what they had done was nothing but their duty to the nation.

I said to the judges that I had no objection if they wanted to represent me without fees. The judges smiled and permitted the great four to file their vakalath namas before the courts which they did. The AG the special prosecutor welcomed the four lawyers telling the court that he was greatly relieved from the ordeal of asking unwanted questions to the person who defended the public interest but standing unfortunately as the defendant.

The Prosecution started his case once again without interruption.

" sir, please tell the court who are you and how you are connected to this case against you?"

One of the four started to say something when I pleaded with eyes not to say anything then.

" I am a retired bank officer. I stay in my son's flat outside the city on the Old mahapalipuram road. I am an author of books. " suddenly I felt something wrong with me. I wanted to say everything about the power of mantra in the court and how I planned and completed my mission on the previous night. But in the court to the question by the persecutor I was not able to tell anything- I tried my level best to recollect but there was nothing that I could remember except that I came to court to attend a case against me .

On seeing me fumbling and confused, the prosecutor repeated the question- carefully avoiding arrogance and the tone of authority which was normal for any prosecutor. But I tried my level best to think and reply. I shook my head violently and tried to restore my memory power. Once I failed- I looked at the persecutor and then the judges and said-

" your honor- I am not able to recollect anything about the case. I came here to tell something – but now suddenly everything gone from my memory. I don't know how and why? " I was highly agitated and tensed without knowing the reason.
The judges asked the prosecutor whether he wanted to continue the case or permit the defendant time to recover from his sudden loss of memory. The AG gladly agreed to post pone the hearing on any suitable date convenient to me. The case was adjourned and I was back in my place in the police HQ.

The whole night I was sleepless and my family members were pestering the police to see me as I was acting strangely in the court. But I told them that I wanted sometime to be alone to think. However much I struggled to get back what I have lost from my memory I could not think beyond my normal life .

Hence I told the police officer who was security in charge of the place where I was kept to take me to the best neuro-specialist to find out what was wrong with me and why I did not remember anything beyond my family life. The DGP came personally to talk to me what exactly I wanted. When I explained to him that there was memory loss for me and I needed a specialist to find out what happened to my brain.

Things moved fast and I was taken to the best neuro physician and was checked thoroughly- keeping me there for a few days. At the end of the investigation, I was found to be normal and my brain was working normally and there was no indication of any damage to any part of the brain or spinal chord.

I was sent back to the police HQ to my usual place.

The hearing was getting delayed because of my inability to remember anything. But the prosecution was pressurized by those who were against me to put me on the stand to find out whether I was lying or why I was lying or acting as if I had selective amnesia like the movie characters. I was taken again to the court since the prosecution could not keep quiet without valid reasons.

Again the AG asked me the same question about my connection to the punishment so many VVIPs in a cruel manner. I was confused and the court appreciated my genuine problem. Hence I voluntarily came forward to be subjected to lie-detector test while answering the questions of the prosecution. The judges were taken aback on my request for a lie test. But I told them that more than the persons who were against me I was concerned with my own memory loss. But if I was found lying without my control I wanted me to be given proper medical treatment to prevent from unwanted lying.

My representations were objected to by the four lawyers but I openly pleaded in the court itself that they should not come in the way of my getting the medical care I needed to get back my memory.

On the subsequent hearing elaborate arrangements were made to connect me to a lie detector in the chamber of the courts in the presence of the full bench of judges, top police officers, the four lawyers, the AG and other officials of the persecution, the emissary of the CM. Besides there were specialists to monitor the equipment headed by a renowned psychologist and neuro physician .

My answers were monitored and checked and found to be normal without a trace of lying as the readings indicated that there was no abnormality in my answers. Again and again they repeated the tests with several questions about my involvement in each case of punishment particularly related to those cases punished by me directly. But all the answers were found to be ok . The specialists concluded their tests with a joint statement that I was not lying to any questions by the prosecution or by the judges and I was telling what I knew without suppressing anything.

I was taken back to my police HQ place totally frustrated. I knew something more about the cases against me than what I remembered. But I did not know how to get back my memory . On the next afternoon, without telling me where I was taken to, I was asked to get into the police van. I was asked to get down with the usual police securities and there, I saw the board of Central Bureau of Investigation . I realized that the case had been handed over to the CBI either by the state government or at the request of the central government as there was no progress even after two months from the arrest.

I was taken through a maze of rooms on either sides. Finally in a room fully protected with thick iron grills I was asked to wait . I was standing there under suspended light. After half an hour, three plain clothes men entered and closed the door behind them.

One of them asked me plainly in English- " you have admitted to the crimes when you were arrested. You have obtained the lists of 4683 people whom you have asked to surrender and confess. Out of them you have admitted to have killed 74 just to make others confess all their crimes and you have given open warning to the government and the courts that all the cases of confession should be completed before the dead line fixed by you- do you deny these charges ?"

I did not remember a word of what he said. Hence I replied-

" though what you are telling me now, appear to me the right actions taken –but I do not know or I don't remember whether I was the one who punished the people or killed the criminals."

Another one from the trio retorted – " hello you are an old man- appear to be a hero in the minds of Tamilians –but we are different. We want the truth. We know that you went to the magazine office to thank them for giving you the lists- you wanted. There are seventeen witnesses for the admission of the guilt by you . We do not know why the Tamilnadu police treat you like a VIP when you have committed atrocities in the name of punishing the criminal while yourself is a grandmaster of the criminals" he was laughing and others also joined him. They were from other states.

I kept quiet when one of the three asked me " whether you needed the same treatment you have given to the criminals to get the truth from you?"

I kept quiet. That was all I remembered. The next few minutes were scenes of punching, thrashing me violently with a cloth covered iron rod or some such thing. I was reeling with pain and became giddy and fell down. But they poured ice water and got me up to demand an admission of all the crimes and also to tell them how I committed them. They wanted the names of those who helped me because they strongly believed that as an old person I could not have punished so brutally those VVIPs without a team of supporters.

I repeatedly told them that I did not remember anything and all I knew was that I was going to tell the court something which I knew about the case but had forgotten at the last moment. They took me into task to the extent possible to spare my life and pushed into the corner and left the room locking from outside.

The torture continued for a week and I was losing weight and health. They were not bothered about me and were focused only their objective of getting the truth from me. On the tenth day after my detention by the CBI. I was taken out to another place- the CBI court where I was presented before a group of top officials of the CBI.

They also asked me the same questions like those who tortured me for ten days. I replied the same thing to them. But they were better than the three persons. On seeing my failing health and knowing that I was having the back up of a state CM and 6 million Tamilians, they told their court official to take me to the hospital and give me the necessary treatment while warning the tree that they had exceeded their powers in reducing a person who was treated as god in big state to the level of a hard core criminal. They pointed out the results of the lie detector and the psycho and neuro specialist reports. The whole world was watching the case with divided interest.

I was taken to the hospital under CBI security staff and it took one month for them to bring back my 70% normal health. Though the broken bones were set, yet, I had lost the 100% usage in my left leg and shoulder. I was told by the attending physician who was my admirer to appeal to the High court for saving me from the cruel hands of CBI. I thanked him and told that everything would be alright in course of time since I believed strongly in goddess Kali.

Once back in the CBI custody I was taken to Delhi as the CBI feared that the people of Tamil nadu might do something to prevent their investigation if I was kept in Chennai. At Delhi, I was treated like third rated hard core criminal and was given the same treatment with a difference- I was kept in a separate room- with a stone bench and dirty looking Indian type- stinking commode. There was black bed sheet and an apology for a pillow- a mud pot with a bent aluminium tumbler with some water.

I could tolerate kicks and other physical tortures but not a foul smelling lavatory –that too- in a place just where I was asked to spend my whole day. I asked Kali why i had to suffer like this for an alleged crimes I had committed about which I could not remember. I just could not sit or sleep and I had not eaten anything from the morning. It was nearing 1 PM in the afternoon.

Till then, I had to eat when I was hungry or else I would feel like vomiting and would get headache. I was a terror to my family members whenever I was on the hungry mode waiting for food. My wife had suffered many times on account of my hunger tantrums and now when I was twitching with hunger, no one cared to listen to me or get me the food I wanted badly. Around 2 PM an aluminum plate containing three stone made rotis with some semblance of side dish with water forming part of the major ingredient and a few pieces of potato. I was just wondering whether other prisoners also were given food like what I got or was it a special food for me alone. I could not take it near my mouth as the smell was repulsing and aggravating the vomiting sensation.

I thought that I was going to die of hunger if I was given the same treatment for a week or so. I tried peep through the grill-gate and saw no one in the vicinity. On one side the crushing hunger and the other the smelling rotten room and I felt like crying aloud. At that time, a tall thin prison guard came and saw that I had not touched the food. He shouted at me to eat or else the consequences. I told him in Hindi that I needed some rice and some cooked vegetables as I was an old man of 68. He scowled at me and asked me to go to hell.

I pleaded to him to at least get me a cup of tea and good water to drink. He took his rifle and simply hit me in my stomach through the gap in the grill gate throwing me backwards to the wall behind. He disappeared with a warning that I should have eaten the food before he came back on his usual round. I got terrible pain in the place where the butt of the rifle hit me and the vomiting sensation added with terrible headache had all joined together to make me faint. I was woken up by a hard stick like thing on my chest and I opened my eyes. I saw two security guards standing over me and demanding me not to act and get up.

I mustered all my remaining strength and raised up to a sitting position. They were shouting at me to stand up and start eating the rubbish food. I saw them and they saw me. That was all. There was a dramatic change in the behaviour of the two. That meant that I got back my powers of the mantra and that was why the two were looking blank at me. I was so happy that tried to recollect from the time I had lost contact with the mantra power. I said to myself " yes – I was in the court room when the persecutor was asking me my connection with the crimes" MY hunger had gone and my headache had disappeared and I was behaving like a child lost in a festival crowd- upon seeing his parents. The two were standing there like statues. The first thing I wanted to test whether I had got back the power of the mantra was to ask them to bring rice, cooked vegetables, tea and a bottle of mineral water- from a good food stall. Further I told the one who was going to bring my requirements that if any one asked him to whom he was taking the food items etc, he should tell them that it was for a prison official. I asked one of them to remain as a guard outside and the other to go and bring my requirements.

They saluted me and the tall one who hit me with the rifle quickly went out and the new one took the position outside my room –but not locking it from outside. I had to wait for half an hour before the prison guard brought sweet smelling hot food from somewhere with a flask full of tea and a bottle of a branded mineral water.

I completed the entire food and gulped two cups of tea and offered the balance to them which they declined politely. I told them to take away the packing materials and dump them somewhere not to be seen by any higher official. Then it struck me – a timely intelligent thought- to ask them whether any one of them had a mobile phone. One of them took out a dainty piece and I asked him to tell how I should dial. He gave the instructions and I told them to go for their usual rounds but should come to me once in fifteen minutes. They shook their heads and went out. The prison room was not locked outside but the lock was simply kept on the hook.

I dialled my residence at Chennai and when I heard my wife's voice after two months I became emotional and something was choking my throat and words did not come out. But she was asking repeatedly who was on the other side. Finally she gave and disconnected. I once gain dialed and that time, I managed to say hello and it was her turn to become emotional and after ten minutes of mutual attack of choking of the throats, I told her I was in Delhi Tihar jail and was alright.

She told me that due to pressure on the government to take some action against me from all sides, the CM had requested the CBI to take the case. That was the reason why I was transferred to CBI custody. She and my other family members were taken to CBI HQ for enquiry and they were drilled for hours and finally when they could not get anything, they were planning to detain them also. But the four lawyers sensing the tricks of the CBI approached the high court to release us as we retained without a prima facie case against my wife and others. In the court, my wife and my family members told what happened during the CBI custody the high court took strong objections to the manner in which my family members were treated even when they were neither alleged criminals nor the CBI had evidences against any one of them. The medias torn the CBI officials into pieces and the lawyers referred the matter to Human rights commission forth with. The CM wrote to PM and the President about the torture of my family members. The CBI came out with an apology with a promise to take suitable action against the officials who exceeded their powers.

The media gave the information that I was taken to Delhi for further enquiry and she was worried what they would do to me. Already a doctor had told the medias that I was tortured by the CBI and was under treatment for severe physical injuries at the hospital for a month and I refused to refer the matter to the court and human rights commission despite his offer to help me. The four leading supreme court lawyers jumped on that press release by the doctor and filed a habeas corpus petition in the High court. The petition was posted for hearing on the next week at the Chennai High court. They came to my flat and assured all help to get the release from the case and my wife had nothing to fear for my life. Even the CM had sent a minister to console my wife and family members besides thousands of social organizations and well known social workers including internationally famous writer of West Bengal, the 'people safety' movement woman social worker of Gujarat- Tamilnadu think tank- Ramamritham, retired judges, DGPs and even the present DGP and commissioner all came to my flat to express their support to me and to my family members.

Fearing unexpected attacks on my family members, in front of my flat complex, a temporary police post was established with ten police gun wielding constables under the head of a senior sub inspector. That was in addition to a group of young men under the banner of "Save the soul who saved the state" numbering around thirty who had stationed outside the flat complex under a tent. They had taken upon themselves to protect my family and fight for my release. My wife said that there were three lakh volunteers to the movement and the numbers were increasing in the Tamilnadu –particularly the college students and the employed youth. They were getting the support from all the sections – low-middle and upper class people – that too from all the districts. She asked not to worry about her and other family members. The case filed in the Human rights commission was posted at the end of the month. But she was crying to see that I had been in prison at Delhi.

I did not tell her about my recent retrieval of the mantra effect as I feared that my phone connections might have been eavesdropped. But I simply told her not to worry about me as Kali had given me enough strength to withstand any amount of problems from any quarters. I hung up and took out the sim card.

Every fifteen minutes the two prison guards were showing their faces. The day was coming to an end and so was the duty of the two. Around 6 pm, they came along with two new tough looking guards who were fretting and fuming for being brought to see a prisoner by force. On seeing them I immediately understood and instantly mesmerized them. The stiffness in their faces had gone and in its place the usual blankness prevailed. I asked the new ones to wait inside my room while I took the old pair outside and told them to forget what they had done –what they talked and what they had seen and asked them to walk away without looking back. I returned the mobile phone without the SIM card without forgetting as it might bring back memory –I did not know. It was because- no one had given me the set of rules and limitations for exercising the mantra power. I was finding out from the usage from the beginning. Before giving the parting instructions , I asked the rifle attacker about the eatery from where he brought the food for me. He said something which I did not understand and hence I called one of the new guards- to get the details from his reliever about the food arrangement. He listened and told me that he knew the place.

Around 8 pm I got my night ration of good chappathi- good side dish- good water. I ate but I could not use the lavatory . Hence I waited patiently till 10 pm when I asked one of the guards who was the officer in charge of the prison where I was kept. He gave the details about my prison block- it was Block No 14- where only hardcore criminals considered as extremely dangerous according to the home department would be kept, It was given the highest security of all the 20 blocks in the Tihar jail like Block No 10 where the VIPs were kept.. The officer in the rank of DIG was in charge and his office was at the northern end of the block 14. I asked him about his personal room and the facilities. He said that it was an air-conditioned room with attached bath room and well maintained by the prisoners.

I thanked him and told him to lock my room keeping the dirty looking bed sheet over the stone bench as if I was sleeping – the lavatory mug as my head and the plate as my foot. I then asked him to carry me to the DIG office. I further instructed him if any one asked why I was taken at that time, he should tell that the duty officer wanted to make some enquiry. He should give the wrong cell number and not mine because I did not want all the securities to be brought under the spell of the mantra.

It was ten thirty in the night- when the lights were switched off except the one in between the rows of prison cells. The prisoners were expected to go to sleep compulsorily. I closed my face with my shirt and with my bare body I behaved as if I was ill and was taken out for some treatment. I wanted to be always cautious and that only helped me when the police found out who the unknown force was. On the way, I got down at one or two places to give rest to the guard who was carrying a dead weight of 100 kgs. Fortunately we did not encounter any unwanted questions from other prison guards and after ten minutes- tough-going through several small lanes, we finally reached a separate enclosure guarded by prison guards. I got down from the guard and acted as if I was not able to stand. My escort told them that I became sick and the duty officer wanted to talk to me, giving a wrong cell number as instructed by me and hence he was taking me inside. They looked at me from head to foot and asked both of us to wait. He told the other guards to take care of us and went inside probably to ask permission for us to meet the officer at that time of the night when he might be taking rest.

He was angry when he came back telling my escort that the officer did not ask for meeting any sick prisoner –however he continued to say that the officer wanted to see who the escort and the sick prisoner he wanted to meet at that time.   He then seized the rifle from the escort and shouted at him to take the prisoner to the duty officer after frisking me and the escort as well. There was no reaction in the behavior of the escort and I was carried once again . I acted as if I was afraid of the sentries shouting. I got down at the entrance of the room   and once inside the big spacious room, I saw an uniformed senior officer-under the influence of liquors who asked the escort to tell him whether he ever asked him to bring a prisoner at that time of the night for enquiry. He then looked at me and that was all for him. He was brought under my control and asked him to go and wash his face and stop acting like a drunken fool. He went inside the bathroom and came back after doing what I had told him to do. I asked the guard to go and tell the sentry to come and see the officer. When he came I told the officer to tell him that he only gave the orders to bring me at that time. He saluted and left .

I told the escort to go and have deep sleep at the corner. Then I asked the officer whether the bathroom was neat and clean. He nodded to say that it was clean. I then told him to go to sleep and went to use the bath room which I have been waiting to do from the afternoon. Once I was happy to have downloaded what I had accumulated, I woke up the officer and told him about the Tihar jail and where those VVIP and VIP criminals were lodged and what was the security arrangement and who managed the entire prison and where was the main office and how many officers would be there at each block etc.

He gave a clear picture of the inner details of the biggest prison of the country- which at that time was keeping 23 VIP criminals –many of them under trail alleged criminals – involved in mega frauds- misappropriation, a Pakistani spy, two captured terrorists who attacked armed HQ killing many soldiers and a major, foreign national involved in molesting 17 children, an underground mafia leader, an ex-MP- a dacoit leader- the terror of Bihar- having 139 criminal cases against him- ex-minister who master minded the fertilizer scam running to three thousand crores in Uttar Pradesh, a female Meghalaya Minister who was found to have been involved in arms smuggling to the insurgency outfits- one central minister who managed to pocket 1690 crores of rupees from an international sports events conducted in India- two Tamilnadu political leaders involved in the biggest single fraud which had shaken the nation on seeing the magnitude of the corruption behind the fraud. There were 12 direct VIPs and 11 government officials and businessmen who were accomplices and beneficiaries of the mega irregularities committed by the political leaders. I asked him to prepare the list and give to me- which he did within a few minutes. I kept it in my pant pocket.

He told me that the VIPs were kept in the most secured fortress like block – No 10-with two DIG level officers taking turns to be in-charge of the block. There were nearly fifty five guards keeping 24 hours vigil—he concluded. I asked him who would be there at that time of the night -11 pm in charge of the block . He gave a name and said that between 10 pm to 6 am- a senior SP would be there to look after the block and the DIGs would take over from 6 am to 10 pm only.

I then asked the officer to get me as many new or old ball pens , which he did within a few minutes-opening all the table and desk drawers. I asked him to keep them in his pant pockets and give them to me when I asked for them. I then casually told him to take me to the block 10, He did not hesitate and started immediately and I followed him faithfully. We went in the flood lit- open court yards well guarded by night duty prison constables –some of them wielding rifles and others –lathis in their hands. After fifteen minutes walking in the open areas, he stopped before a barbed wire entrance with sentries on either side. On seeing him both the guards saluted and waited for his orders. He told them that he was asked to come to meet the SP with me without telling who I was. They simply let him inside with me but I was acting as if I was wiping my face with a towel which I pilfered from the bathroom of the officer when I went to use the bathroom.

Once inside the big open area around a massive four story building- the block no 10- I presumed, the officer went quickly to the opposite side of the entrance and stopped in front of a small building forming part of the block. The sentries there also saluted him and allowed us to enter and I had to same trick of the towel wiping face and we entered a small ante room where the officer stopped and knocked another door. After some time the door was opened and a bulk of a man with half uniform appeared at the threshold. On seeing the officer, " hello- Puri sab- what brings you here- come- come" he must be a friend of the officer who must also be in the SP rank- I thought. On seeing me tagging along with his colleague, our eyes met and at the same time he came under my control. He asked me also to come inside.

Once we three sat down- the SP at his usual official chair and we two on the chairs meant for visitors- I asked the officer to handover the pens which he was keeping with him. He gave a bunch of pens which I kept them on the table. I then asked him to go back to his office and sleep there till I came to wake him up. He said "yes" and I saw the SP with a smile. He looked without expressions at me. I asked him whether he had a photo copier in his office. He replied in affirmative. I then asked him whether he had A-4 size blank papers and extra new ball pens. He said they were available in the office attached to his room. I asked who was holding the keys to the prison cells under his control. He showed a steel cupboard and told me that they were kept safely inside the bureau.

I then asked him to call for a prison guard. He did and I mesmerized him when our eyes met. I then asked the SP to open the bureau containing the keys. He replied like at a bullet speed that the key for the bureau was under the custody of the DIG. I asked him where the DIG kept the keys over night. He told me that he had kept in his office next to his but he could not open it without permission from the DIG. I told him to open it as it was an emergency and he opened his cupboard and took out a leather jacket and took out a bunch of keys from the purse like thing. I then asked him to open the office and bring the prison cells keys pertaining to only the 23 VIPs – the list I already got it prepared by the officer of my block 14- and those connected with them. I told the prison guard to help the SP . They both went out while I checked the fridge in the room- for something to drink. There were only liquors inside and three bottles of branded mineral water. Wearing the towel over my hand - I opened one of them and drank half of it and wiped the outside carefully before replacing it in the same place. I waited for twenty minutes when one of the VIP criminals appeared at the door step and when i saw him and when he saw me- the matter was over and I asked him to sit down on the floor at the corner. Within a few minutes another one appeared – I did the same thing with him also and he was asked to sit next to the person sitting already. Thus within an hour- all the twenty three VIPs and their accomplices were made to sit in the available space .

I then asked the SP to get me a bunch of blank papers and the spare ball pens- in his office. He got my requirements. I asked the prison guard to give four sheets per VIP with a pen. But the pens were not adequate and I told the SP to bring additional supply from the DIG room. Even then they were not sufficient . Suddenly I remembered about the pens the officer had brought. The pocket were found under the chair where the officer was sitting for a few minutes. With them , every one of the 23 got a pen and blank papers to write. I saw the time. It was 12.10 am.

I asked the prison guard and the SP to go to sleep. They sat down on the available chair and started sleeping. I asked the 23 criminals to first admit

134

the crimes they had committed and then write down briefly what they had done and how they done and where they had hidden the ill-gotten money and who were all helped them. They all started earnestly except the Pakistani prisoner and the ex-MP dacoit leader. They were blinking. But I left the two to remain idle while the rest of the 21 were busy in pouring out their heart in confessing to the crimes. I wished to cover the scene by video camera. But where to go for such a facility in the midnight – in the biggest well protected prison at Delhi?

Around 1-20 am, the first female VIP criminal from Meghalaya looked at me to signify that she had completed her job. I asked her to write the confession notes of the ex-MP and told the ex-MP to tell her what she had to write. They both started doing their work- earnestly. Then I took the confession notes of the female criminal and woke up the prison guard to get the copies photo-copied. When he said that he did not know where the photo copy machine was, I showed the copier machine which was already switched on by the SP before he was asked to go to sleep. There were enough blank sheets kept ready near the machine. I told him how to take the copies and he followed my instructions carefully. Within the next ten minutes five other confessions were ready. I got them photocopied. I told one of the criminals who had completed the job I gave him- to write confession notes of the Pakistani criminal.

Thus before 2 am the entire work was over. I asked the prison guard to hand over the photocopies of the confession notes to each one of the 23 criminals and asked them to hold them tightly in their hands. The followed my instructions faithfully. I then woke up the SP and asked him how many bullets were ready for firing in his service revolver. He checked and told me that there were six ready in his gun. I asked whether he had unused cartridges with him and he said 'yes'. I asked him to take out another 18 immediately. He opened a safe inside the steel cupboard where the keys were kept –and from inside he took out a tin box containing the spare cartridges. Fortunately each box contained 24 cartridges and I asked him to remove 18 from and keep the balance in the box itself and close the bureau and lock it securely

I then asked the prison guard to bring all the sentries outside the office and the entrance one by one quickly. He did and one by one- I brought them under my control. There were seven of them near the office of the SP- the rest of them were in the main block guarding the cells.

I told them all to check whether all the window and doors were closed and if not I asked to lock them inside. They did. The SP room was already air-conditioned and must be sound proof also. But as a measure of abundant caution, i asked the SP to get me the sofa cushions if any or pillows from somewhere. He said that only from the DIG 's office he could get .what I wanted. I asked two guards to help him to get what I wanted immediately. Time was running out for me. He came back with two guards carrying ten pieces of thick sofa cushions and two pillows.

I asked all the eight body guards to stand in a row. I told the SP to go to deep sleep. I then asked all the 23 criminals to stand in a row facing the only cement concrete wall. Only 10 criminals could stand side by side facing the wall. I asked the rest to go to sleep and I selected one guard and told the rest to go to sleep. I checked up once again for any door or window open. Once I was satisfied, I asked the guard to take the pistol from the SP which he did. I told the 10 prisoner to keep the cushion covers over their chest and go to deep sleep. When I was satisfied that they were not aware of a thing in the world, I asked the guard to go near the 10 criminals and shoot one by one through the chest quickly without stopping for a second. The echo of the shots were muffled but still could be heard from a distance as something like a cracker noise. I ignored the risk and once all the six shots were fired- I asked the guard to go to sleep and woke the next one to load the pistol with the spare cartridges. He did what t told him. Then I asked him to do the same thing like the first guard. He completed his job well. Again the muffled noise could have been heard outside. My time was running out and I must act quickly. I asked the second guard to go to sleep and woke up the next one and repeated what I told the first two. Thus within 25 minutes, all the twenty three VIP criminals who were kept in prison getting first class treatment trying to prolong the cases against them deliberately with a view to get a bail and eventually free from the criminal charges leveled against them in due course – perhaps till their natural end of life. But they were punished by Kali and they could not escape this punishment impossible to escape- because the court was not constituted by Indian constitution or law and the judge was not a government and parliament appointed person. Here only truth only would be accepted and the policy of crime and punishment was beyond manipulation with power, influence and money.

I asked all the guards to forge what they had seen heard or done till then and asked them to go to sleep and woke up the SP and told him to take me to Block No 14 immediately without looking here and there. He opened the doors and as demanded by me- took me to the Block no 14- I followed him keeping my face covered with the towel as if I was wiping my face. There were no guards on the way to have seen us by chance. Once I was inside the office of the officer in charge of the block -14, I asked the SP to forget what he had seen, heard or done and go back to his office and have a deep sleep without looking here and there. He agreed and left.

I woke up the officer in charge and told him the usual forget instructions and asked him to go to deep sleep once again. Then I woke up the guard who was asked to sleep at 10 .30 pm and told him to carry me back to my cell. Why I wanted to be carried from my cell to office and back was to avoid being found by the sniffer dogs if deployed after finding out the killings of the VIP and my presence in the Tihar Jail at that time. The time was 3.20 am. Before leaving the air-conditioned room of the officer I took a stomach full of good water and something to eat- but there was nothing in the fridge in the officer's room also.

The very thought of remaining in the foul smelling room was revolting. Hence I asked the guard to stand at the entrance to row of cells in my section to tell me whether someone was coming. He saluted and stood at a distance while I remained outside the cell enjoying the morning breeze of the September Delhi weather. I had slept without my knowledge and was woken up by the guard to tell that his duty time would be over in a few minutes. I quickly got inside my cell and the guard locked my cell and took the key to the office room.

At 6 am I was waiting for some guard to turn up. But no one came my side of the prison. I got no tea or I could not clean my teeth etc. Fortunately I had no pressure to go to bath room. Around 8 am a few guards were running outside my cell –shouting something. The cell doors were opened and all the prisoners were brought to the centre of the block. I was also taken to the place along with the hardcore criminals who were looking like the fighters of the WWW programs.

Hundreds of prison guards were surrounding us and top officials were there to see us being checked by the officer in charge- a DIG – and not the one who was holding charge on the previous night. The guards checked us thoroughly and when I was about to be checked I saw deliberately the eyes of guard and brought him under my control . I had to because I was keeping the originals of the confession notes inside my underwear. I smiled at him and he did and I told him to do something for namesake and go to the next person. His actions could not been seen by any official. I heaved a sigh of relief .

Then we were taken to our cell and locked inside safely. But there was a big commotion everywhere in the entire Tihar jail. I could not get to know the details. I told myself that I had to wait patiently. Around 10 am two slices of hard bread and some a dry snack with a plantain were served in my aluminum plate and I could not even look at it leave alone to eat them. I had to wait. At 11 am three persons in plain clothes came to see me and without asking me anything, they left me. Later I came to know that they were from CBI office who came to make a routine check of the prisoner under their control.

Around 12 noon I saw the first guard passing outside my cell. I shouted at him to stop and come see a bunch of currency notes in my room which was thrown through the window of my cell from outside. He stopped for a moment and came back to me asking what I was telling about notes etc. I told him to come inside to see a bundle of 100 rupees lying on the floor. He said that he would come back and went to get the keys to open my cell to check whether there was a bundle of notes. I did not expect him to get the keys in view of the commotion from the morning in the jail. But he returned back quickly with another senior guard and both of them opened my cell in haste. I was laughing at their foolishness to believe me because of their lust for easy money. Once I saw them and they saw me- the curtains fell for their memory.

I told the senior of the two to get me fresh mineral water bottle and good food for me as I was hungry with a specific instruction that if one asked him where he was taking the food, he should tell that it was for an officer without naming him. He nodded his head and I told the other one to visit my cell once in thirty minutes regularly till the reliever came in the evening. He said 'yes sir". I waited for the food and it came after forty minutes in a cloth bag. The food was normal and the water was fresh. I took my lunch but I could not sleep in the wretched cell. I told the senior to forget etc and asked him to go back to his duty place. I closed the cell door and came out and rested on the pillar of the verandah of the cell- as there were no cells in front of the section of the cells where I was kept. It was an open space facing trees and a lawn not maintained – with bushes found everywhere.

I was seeing the guard once in half an hour and I told him to wake me up if someone came to check. I wished to sleep but not deeply and the mantra effect helped to get the rest I needed as I was awake throughout the previous night.

I might have slept for two hours when the guard woke me up to tell that he was going for lunch for half an hour. I asked that he should bring good tea after taking lunch. I gave the same instruction to him that if someone asked him for whom he was taking the tea- he should say that it was for an officer without naming the person. He left and I slept for another 30 minutes. I woke up myself and waited for a few minutes when the guard brought the tea in a vessel but it was hot. I took it and told him to continue his visits once in half an hour till the end of his duty. Casually I asked him whether he had a mobile. He gave me his mobile and like the previous day- the guard taught me how to operate it. I thanked him and once he had left- I dialed my house at Chennai.

My daughter in law took the phone and she started crying on hearing my voice after a long time. I had to pacify her and told her to call my wife quickly as the connection might be cut at any time. She called my wife to come quickly and I heard my wife on the line.

" how are you and the children? " I asked her.

" The TVs are full of news about the killing of 23 VIP criminals in the Tihar jail with confession notes in their hands unlike those who were punished in Tamilnadu. " she wanted me to ask her whether I was behind the killing.

I showed surprise in my voice – but she appeared to have not believed me. But she did not press me and I did not volunteer to tell.

" here the news papers are full of your return back to the punishment program. Medias told – that all those who were crying for the arrest and trial of an innocent old man were shocked by the news of the killing at the jail where the old man was kept under tight security. The jail authorities confirmed that there was no involvement of the prisoner from Chennai whose presence in the cell was confirmed and no evidence to implicate him in that mass killing according to the Tihar jail officials. The medias clearly emphasized that the unknown force had again started its activities after a temporary rest of a few months. It would certainly take up the cases of those who rose against the innocent old man. The 'save the soul who saved the state' group outside my flat complex fired crackers to celebrate the re-emergence of the unknown force at Delhi and they demanded that I should be released from the jail as the killings took place right inside the highest security prison of the nation and I got a clearance certificate from the jail officials.

In the meantime, the Tamilnadu government announced the withdrawal of the case against me and the High Court had given top priority for the case and it would be heard on the next day. The same team of lawyers would represent me as per the information from my wife. But I was wondering how the Tihar official could come to such a conclusion that I was not involved in the killing without making any enquiry with me. I did not understand but suddenly felt after some deep thought over the strange behavior of the officials that their future depended on my future. If they said that I might be behind the killing – only they had to explain as to how I could do it when there were hundreds of gun wielding guards were there round the clock and how the killings could be possible right under their presence and how they did not remember to have seen the killing and how they facilitated the killer to open the office of the DIG, to take out the keys to special cells of the VIP, to give the unused cartridges to the killer and how the guards fired the shots with the service revolver of the SP and how the confession notes were photo copied from the ,machine kept in the SP office and what happened to the originals of the confession notes.

The nation shook with the confession notes as if it was struck by a violent earth quake- because- the confession notes would help to nab the real criminals besides those who were in the jail and shot, to confiscate the huge hidden money , to get a clear picture of how the frauds took place from the beginning. The killing was a shock to the public but more than that – the confession notes- killed the public trust in the government machinery. Everywhere there were agitation and public demand for immediate action on the basis of the confession and also to get the originals of the notes immediately. As usual in all the states except Tamilnadu – medias demanded to get the bottom of the killing spree and to arrest the culprits. Tamilnadu medias announced the return of the Unknown force – at Delhi.

It was time for the change of guards. But no one came to me and the new guard did not come like yesterday. I was worried about my dinner and the stinking cell which was not locked and I was remaining outside freely-bitten by the mosquitoes. It was past 7 pm when I saw a guard at a distance coming towards me. I thought for a moment whether to get inside the cell or remain outside. I did not want to take a risk of the guard not seeing me inside the cell. Hence I stood there away from the cell and he almost came running towards me. Before he could ask something, his eyes met mine and there he stood mesmerized.

I asked him whether he was the reliever of the day duty guard. He said 'yes'. I told him to go and bring good food and a bottle of mineral water for me as I was hungry. I told him the usual advice to tell that the food was for the officer without giving the name. He obeyed my orders. I waited outside the cell taking shelter under the cover of the big pillars of the building on the verandah. The mosquito menace was more in the cell than outside- at least outside there was good air circulation and there was no stinking smell of the bed sheet and the lavatory.

After half an hour, the guard returned with two more guards appearing to be officers. They came in quick march and saw me . I saw them and they came under my control. I asked the guard about the food. He looked blinking. I then asked one of the new comers what happened to my food. They did not reply but they were also blinking. Then I told the guard to go for his rounds and come back to see me every thirty minutes positively. He saluted and left. I then asked one of the new comers to go and bring good food with a bottle of mineral water while asking the other one to go inside the cell and sleep. Both the persons did what I asked them to do. After twenty minutes, nice smelling parathas with good side dishes were brought along with a bottle of water. I took my dinner slowly right under the nose of the new comer. Once I took my dinner and belched loudly after consuming water as usual I gave him the parting instructions to forget etc and woke the sleeping one and gave him similar advice and asked both of them to resume their duties. They saluted and left.

I sat down on the verandah and leaned over the pillar and closed my eyes. Every thirty minutes the guard would faithfully carried out my orders and woke me up to salute me. That game continued till 10.30 pm when the lights were switched off in all cells and like previous night, I had planned a program for tonight also. The guard came on his usual round and I told him to see who was in charge of the block that night. He came back to tell me that only DIG was there with ten guards around his office .He added on his own that everywhere there were additional guards than the usual ones. He felt that what happened the previous night might have resulted in the increase of guards in all the blocks.

I did not know how to manage a crowd of 10 guards and the chances of meeting some of the additional guards while on my mission programmed for that day. I thought deeply for some time and the guard was waiting for my orders- either to go or remain. I had an idea. I told the guard under waiting to go and bring one by one the ten guards around the office of the DIG telling that he had seen just then -someone hiding behind a pillar in the open corridor while he was doing his usual rounds. He told me that there were other guards doing the rounds in other sections of the building and he could take their help. I appreciated the working of his mind- despite my mantra effect .

I then told him that to tell one of the guards- that prisoner wanted to say something about the previous night's killing. I asked to add that the prisoner received a call to his mobile phone just then. The guard went and returned with not one- but four duty guards of the DIG office- they were actually running towards me. But I changed my cell position and stood before another cell- three numbers before my cell number. I then asked the duty guard to go on his usual round.

I saw them and all of them saw me in the dim light of the passage. It took a few seconds only to master them and they stood there like statues. I asked one of them to go and bring the rest of the six guards. He saluted and went. The crowd of seven guards were too much for me. But I had to use the mantra or else curtains for me. They were shouting and coming towards me and I stood under the light to enable them to look at me at a distance and when their eyes met mine, all the ten guards came under control. I told two of them to carry me to the DIG office till they reached the door to the air-conditioned room of the top grade officer. His office was next to the room of the officer yesterday. After the killing of the previous night the DIGs were asked to take over the night duty.

I knocked the door and with a grumbling like a bull-dog the jailor peeped out through the half open door and demanded to know what was the matter. I had a fleeting chance to see his drunken eyes and he succumbed to the mantra effect instantly. I asked him to open the door and he did. I went inside asking the 10 guards to sit down and sleep –in the sitting posture- near the door of the DIG.

I then closed the door and asked the DIG to get me the details of the inmates of the 120 cells under his control. He went through the records and got me a heavy register looking like hotel registration book. I asked him to select the worst cases of dreaded criminals who should have been hung but who were managing to prolong the cases against them or staying in the cells with the support of the politicians in first class comforts. He went through the names of three hundred seventy including me in the register and took one hour to finalize the list with 58 top grade criminals who should be eliminated- but who could not eliminated with the present system of justice- he made those comments on his own. In the meantime I used his bathroom to relieve my intestines.

I asked him whether he had a big knife like that of a butcher's. He said 'no'. I asked whether he could get it from somewhere. He said that he could send the guards to get it from the kitchen if required. I said that I required but I told him to go and get it without sending the guards as it would create some unwanted queries by the kitchen staff. He agreed and went out. Meantime I covered my hand and opened the fridge and found nothing by half and full liquors and some bottles of mineral water. I took a bottle with me and kept it in my pant pocket for use at a later stage of the mission.

The DIG came back and showed me the big long knife with shining blade used by the kitchen for cutting the mutton etc. I asked him who was holding the keys of the cells. He said that his subordinate officer in the next office held the keys. Normally the keys in other jails would be with the guards but in the blocks 10 and 14 only the keys would be under the custody of the officer on duty. I asked him to go and bring the officer which he did and within five minutes an officer was brought by the DIG along with a big box of keys –the officer was hypnotized or mesmerized by me on the spot. I felt that on that night I had been bringing more and more people under the mantra effect just for completing the mission successfully.

The officer when he saw the DIG at his room must have been rattled and hence he was not dressed properly. No one cared. I then asked the two DIG and the officer to take me to the cells of the 58 top grade criminals who were escaping punishment. I asked the DIG to bring the knife keeping it behind his shirt. They obeyed my orders and took me outside –jumping over the sleeping guards. The officer was leading us – followed by the DIG and I was in the rear end. The ground floor of the main building had several wings with three floors. The officer now and then checking the list prepared by the DIG, took us to the third cell at the first turning on the ground floor. He opened the cell and went inside to wake up the prisoner number no-226. He was alone in the cell. He was the body guard of a

142

famous politician who killed the bridegroom and raped the bride right under the nose of those who attended the function. His associates were looting the place depriving the jewelry and cash and other valuable from the guests and from the parties to the marriage.

His case was dismissed for want of evidence at high court of Rajasthan and an appeal to supreme court got the criminal a life sentence. He had already completed six years and there was a pressure from the political benefactor- to give him credit for the remissions. Most probably he would be released within two years at the most.

He opened his eyes when he was woken up around midnight. He thought that he was going to be released and hence grinned widely saluting clumsily at the officer and the DIG. When he saw me I had did my job. There was no time to waste.   I asked the criminal to lie on his face exposing his back to us and go to deep sleep, He did. I asked the officer to take the knife from the DIG and plunge it deep inside the area where the heart was. Not once but three times deeply. He did and the DIG did not react. The body convulsed for a few seconds and stopped.   The whole operation took six minutes and I had to take the remaining cases -57. I did not have time. Hence, asked the two officers to quicken the process and complete each stabbing within three minutes on an average. They nodded their heads. the cell was locked with the bleeding body and we marched on to the next in the list. The cell was only a few yards away from the first one. There were two criminals inside and I had mesmerize the two and the officer had to stab them to death quickly.

That process continued for three hours thirty five minutes- before we could complete my mission. We had to go to all the wings and all the floors. Two of the criminals listed were in the same wing where I was kept. In all not 58 but 79 criminals were killed- some of them were like freebies for the dreaded criminals –they were the cell-mates and we had to do the job of punishing in the cell only and I felt that all the criminals in the hardcore criminal block deserved to be hung or killed. But due to paucity of time and my eagerness not to miss the opportunity I did what I could within the safest period of the night. That was upto 4 am.

I told the two officers once inside the DIG office to forget what they had seen, heard or done before asking them to go to deep sleep- the DIG in his room and the officer in his room. The keys were restored to the usual place. The knife was thrown inside a deep gutter on the backside of the building which would become impossible for anyone to retrieve- because the drainage water flow was like at Ganges at Haridwar speed. It might have been carried away from the spot of crime.

I woke up the ten guards and told them to follow my usual instructions of forgetting etc and told nine out of them to go to deep sleep and the last one to carry me to my cell. I told him to bring the usual guard on duty to me and he did. Once the guard of my wing came there, I repeated my usual instructions to him and told him to go and join his colleagues and sleep deeply. I told the guard to keep me inside the cell, lock the door, take the keys and leave. He did with a salute.

At around six in the morning I woke up- I slept with the mantra effect in that wretched place and waited for the duty guard to appear. The waiting was prolonging and there was like the previous day, commotion and running of guards here and there but no one to my wing. But suddenly a team of officers and guards were coming towards my wing. I went into deep sleep once again.

I was forcibly woken up by the butt of a rifle and there I saw several faces looking at me. They asked me to get up and I struggled to stand immediately- but I was pulled violently and was thrown outside. I managed to balance myself. I saw a crowd in front of the third cell where we had killed one of the listed criminals. I was pushed by the guards and without allowing me to see what happened I was taken to the big open space where I found my building mates standing in rows. I was asked to take a place and there – I saw a dozen DIGs, IGs and other senior officers looking frightened with anger overpowering them like patients suffering from epilepsy.

Dogs were deployed to do their part of the investigations and they were taken to each remaining prisoner. I did know whether the mantra effects were restricted to humans or to animals also. But my fate would be decided by the dogs if only they caught me to show that I was the culprit. Whatever precaution I might have taken – the body smell of mine could not be removed. But I managed the foot prints by wearing the shoes of the DIG who was like my physically. But I soaked the shoes after the use in water and threw them in an attic like place inside the bathroom.

When the dog came to the next prisoner, frantically I tried to look at its eyes and only when it was my turn to be sniffed, the eye to eye was possible and I prayed for the effect sincerely. I wished the dog to sniff but not to do anything else and should go to the next prisoner. It did what I wished and I escaped from certain end of my mission. But the sniffer dog's investigation was over, we were frisked by the guards who checked our dress and body and the limbs for blood spots. I took the precaution of remaining outside the cells when the stabbing was done by the officer and the DIG alternatively. Their dresses were full of tell-tale marks of blood.

Once cleared by the direct investigation by the dogs and the guards we were taken back to the cells and pushed inside it –duly locked outside by the guards.

I had to wait for the day to move on as I had no other plans at that moment. I was feeling hungry and had to wait for the usual guards on rounds. But knowing what had happened the previous day, I was not sure whether I would be lucky to get food leave alone good food. 79 prisoners stabbed to death and two jailors involved in the killing – the news must have been another bombshell for the government and like 11000 KW electric shock for the people.

No guard came to the wing till lunch time when at last a guard came with my prison lunch and threw it through the gap between the floor and the cell iron door when I frantically tried to see him. But he simply pushed the plate and left without seeing me. I shouted that there was no water from the night to drink. He hesitated for sometime before returning back to get the pot. That was sufficient for me. The small opening in the grill gate through which the prisoners requirements were to pushed inside was sufficient for the pot also. I emptied the dirty water in the commode .While I was squeezing through the pot through the opening, I saw him and he saw me and he became my man-Friday from that second. I asked him to go and get me good vegetarian food with a bottle of mineral water from somewhere and if any asked him about the food, I told him to tell that it was for an officer. Knowing the commotion and tension outside, I asked him to hide the food carefully and bring it safely to me.

He saluted and gone .I waited for ages. After an hour's time, he came carrying a bag which he gave it to me through the opening. Inside there was a neatly packed food items and a bottle of good drinking water with seal intact. I thanked him and told him to come and see me once in 30 minutes. He saluted and left. Between the previous day and today, the difference was – the place of taking the lunch. Inside the cell, I forcibly forgot the smell and the atmosphere and took the not so hot food and took the bottle of water fully. The belching gave the signal for me to sleep irrespective of the surroundings.

I kept the packing material and the bag inside the bed sheet along with the original confession notes-kept in a polythene covers. I then used the mantra and slept deeply- I did not for how long when I was woken up by someone. I opned my eyes and I could not believe my eyes. There before me were the DGP of Tamilnadu, one of the four lawyers, someone looking like a party functionary- and a bunch of police officers – all from Tamilnadu.

They all saluted me and helped me to get up. They asked to leave the dirty cell immediately and once outside, the DGP introduced me to the dhoti clad person- he was the minister for social welfare – the pet of the CM. He shook hands with me –deviating from the practice of folded hands –the trade mark of Tamilnadu politicians. The minister explained to me that the High court had accepted the plea of the Tamilnadu government to withdraw the cases and they declared that I was a free man and hence I should not detained in any custody. They talked to CBI office of Tamil nadu representative who appeared in the court to inform their HQ to release the alleged criminal forthwith. There was no objection from the CBI side and once everything was clear, the CM asked the minister to take the team of top police officers, and the lawyers by a chartered flight to bring back me to the state immediately

The DGP added that the news of killing of 79 hardcore criminals in the Tihar jail – a second in succession of killing by unknown force- simply shattered the CBI's confidence in their powers and hence the release was made within s few minutes by the top officials. Further, the Delhi police also were literally torn into pieces by the massive killing of prisoners in the tightest security prison. They did not know what to do and where to look. The blood stains in the dress of the DIG and the SP proved conclusively that they were the ones who committed the barbaric stabbings till death of the criminals. But they did not remember a thing about the crimes- but the kitchen staff clearly told that the DIG came and took a butcher's knife and did not return it to him. There were ten guards and no one remember anything about the killing or the DIG or the SP leaving their offices. But to top of all the strange things that took place on the night, why none of the 79 criminals cried or protested or fought or counter attacked the two officers when they were stabbing them repeatedly. They were all killed like sacrificial goats during the festivals in the villages. Why they remained silent and meekly accepted the punishment?

The top officials and the government home department, the ministers, the PM, and even the President were all confused over the manner in which the killings were committed for two days in succession that too inside the prison and further by the officials who were supposed to be in charge of the prison blocks. The medias were making their own guesses and some quoted the similarities with what happened in Tamilnadu sending a warning note to the corrupt politicians and others to be beware as the unknown had landed in the capital to punish those who thought that they had escaped from the crimes they had committed without the fear of punishment.

BY the time the DGP finished briefing me about the after effects of the previous night's punishment program, we had reached the Tamilnadu house- the state guest house. How the media men got the scent – nobody knew could guess- they were there. They demanded an interview with me and I agreed.

" sir, you were kept in the Tihar jail as an accused who had admitted to the killing of several persons in Tamilnadu and now when you were there in the jail many persons were killed like those incidents which took place in your state. Are you going to admit that only you had killed the persons who deserved to be punished. " one of the media person asked me when the video cameras were kept before me – one over the other- fighting for a space to get my voice clear and near.

" I had admitted to the crimes when I felt that I should do. But subsequently I had lost my memory and when I was under CBI control, they brought me to Tihar jail where I was under lock and key from the time I was kept till the Tamilnadu police released me. I cannot reply to your question directly- but – whether I killed or some unknown force killed, those who were punished should be treated as the enemies of the nation. Do you make hue and cry over those who were killed by our jawans or soldiers in the war? Why? You cannot- because they were enemies of the nation. But I would say that they were better than the alien enemies who were killed in the jail. The soldiers of alien army were not criminals nor have they misused their political powers to enrich themselves nor have they raped or murdered people for money- not have they misappropriated the public funds in thousands of crores . Now my dear media persons, do you want them to be brought back to life to save the country which cannot be run without their support? DO you feel that the killing was a murder under Indian Penal code? If your sister or wife was raped and your family members were mercilessly butchered would you ask this question? Just because you were not affected by the hardcore criminals you have asked me the question whether I would admit to the Tihar jail killings like Tamilnadu. DO you want to proceed against my own admission to the massacre. If you from media feel like this, why the jail officials did not raise a finger against me? They brought the sniffer dogs squad to check every one of us- have they obtained any finger prints anywhere connected to me? If they have proof for my involvement why should they release me from the prison? Leave alone the killing of the criminals- why should the criminals themselves confess to the crimes they had committed? Who forced them to confess and why should 79 keep quiet and allow to be stabbed to death? Where do I come in the killing when the evidences pointed out clearly to the DIG and the SP? . Do you know the Tamilnadu government had withdrawn the case against me and the High court of Chennai ordered for my release? Why do not you all file cases against me that I only committed the crimes ?"

I stopped and showed the lawyer standing to my right and said " if someone thinks that I was behind the killing , this supreme court lawyer along with three others would certainly demand a conclusive proof for my involvement? If a group of persons related to those who were killed in the jail could support and represent hardcore criminals why not the lawyers to support a law abiding old man like me   living out of my   pension peacefully? Are you ready?" I forgot I was talking to the national media persons for a moment and became emotional- but I regained my control and quickly toned down my voice   and continued to talk to them –but normally.

" my dear friends- I just got emotional not for the fear of my life –but I felt sorry to see that the country still believed in the legal system to punish the people who considered themselves beyond the control of the laws. My dear friends, I will not stand in the way of anyone complaining against me or filing a court case or start some agitations for action against me. But I am happy to find that at last someone whether it is me or you or some unknown force-   has started punishing those who should have been punished long back. I hear from the media reports that people openly say that they have started living peacefully after many decades."

The media persons looked at the press person who questioned me with annoyance. The senior member of the most popular TV channel said –" sir, what you said is cent percent correct. But for the unknown force no one could have even dreamt about taking action against those powerful criminals backed up money and political leaders. But the question was asked only to make it clear that you could not be the unknown force since the recent killings were reportedly done by the DIG and the SP. We the medias also strongly support the actions of the unknown person or force but we are against the crude manner in which the punishments were meted out to the criminals. Another thing which appears to be foolish now is the question –why we should be talking to you if you were not the unknown force and why we should ask the questions which we should ask only the great invisible punisher? We apologize for this meaningless interview " so saying he left the place followed by the other media persons one by one. They were discussing something between themselves whether to take me as the unknown force or to take my talk seriously and leave as an old man. They looked totally confused and dejected

The Chennai group went inside the big guest home and I was given the VIP suite where only the CMs used to stay while at Delhi. In the big hall like room, I was asked to take rest before taking the night flight to Chennai. They kept some new dresses for me ready and food was waiting for me. I took a hot bath and cleaned myself which I could not for the past two months. I had a good dinner as per the Tamilian menu. Once eaten to the full stomach, I could not go to sleep which I wanted. But I called the DGP to find out whether they had their dinner and rest. The Minister came and told me that the CM was happy that I was released and I was keeping normal health.

We all except the lawyer who had his residence at Delhi boarded the flight to Chennai. I thanked the lawyer and told him that I owed much to him for my release from the jail. He said that it was the duty of all those who called themselves true Indian. The plane landed at 10.45 pm and I was led by the team of DGP, Minister and other officials with police men to the VIP exit where my wife and others were waiting for me. Outside there were thousands of cheerful volunteers of the 'save the soul' group. They were shouting slogans for my long life and the policemen took enormous efforts to put barricades to stop them from entering the VIP lounge.

After talking to my family I went out to address the people in Tamil- who gathered there even at that time-

" My dear Indians, whether I am an unknown force or not, you have accepted me as the savior of the people of this country. I thank you all for the security you had provided to my family when I was in jail. Whether I had punished or someone else punished the deserving criminals, the people should feel happy that the time had come to get the share of the fruits of freedom our mahatmas got us after great struggle in 1947. Only 2% of the entire 102 crores of people are enjoying without worrying about the water, electricity, gas, transport, food, clothes, shelter, cyclone, earth quake, tsunamis, floods, standing in the queue for ration, railway tickets, kerosene, admission in the hospitals, educational institutions and a host of other essentials for the common man to lead a normal life in this country. Rest of the 98% are still under captivity of not under the   alien armed forces or foreign rulers but persons worse than these people- namely Indian politicians and corrupt officials.

What is the reason? The simple answer is the fundamental mistakes in the Indian constitution which was based on British and Irish models. There are no restrictive clauses in the whole of the constitution with the result, today, the same family can rule the country for centuries though every Indian is eligible to become a PM or a CM- only millionaires can contest elections- criminals can become MLA MP or minister or even PM or CM or President Till now no mega frauds were punished and till now no political atrocities were punished- government buses have been burnt- railway carriages were destroyed- hundreds of bomb blasts killing hundreds of innocent people- hundreds of train accidents due to sabotages and human errors- not a single party can boast of a single corrupt free leader. Why? All because of the constitution . hence I am going to start the agitation for revising the constitution to restore the freedom for the common people. I need your support and the support of every Indian. Will you help to achieve my life time wish?" I waved at the crowd- the response was spontaneous – We will- we will "

I promised to meet them later and said good bye to them while being escorted to the waiting big van. Boarded the semi-bus like vehicle fully furnished with my family members after expressing my thanks to the minister, DGP and other officials and the policemen.

That night we all slept only at 4 am I told them about the rough treatment I got from the CBI and the stinking cell in the Tihar Jail.

On the next days, I had met a number of social activists and the VIPs of the state including the visit by the CM. I heard from my elder son that everybody believed that I was the unknown force which was made clear by the killing of the 23 VIP and 79 hardcore criminals when I was there in the same jail. The CM called to assure his full government support as he knew that I was the unknown force.

I went to meet the AG of the state and the chief justice of high court. They were happy to see me back in the state. They did not bother about my involvement with the killings and acted as if I had returned from the war front after defeating the enemies of the nation in a pitched battle. It was after a week when I was talking to a group of students when the news flash appeared in the TV in my drawing room where I was having the meeting.

" 189 feared dead and hundreds seriously injured in the series of bomb blast at the VT station"

I dismissed the meeting with an excuse and rang up the DGP. When he came on the line, I told him to talk to his counterpart at Mumbai that I would like to involve myself directly in this case. I then asked him to book an air ticket to Mumbai in the next available flight and send a vehicle to take me to the airport immediately. He said that he would do it. I also told him that I would talking to the CM also. Then I contacted the personal secretary of the CM to tell the CM that I wanted to talk to him immediately. I got the call from the CM to whom I repeated what I told the DGP. He was happy to know that I wanted to take up the case. He offered to do anything I wanted. I asked him to talk to the CM of the state to cooperate with me . He promised to do it then and there.

After an hour's wait the police car came and a SP rank officer told me that the car and the tickets were ready for me and that I would be accompanied by him along with two commandos in civilian dress. I did not bother to hear the details. What prompted me to punish the criminals from the beginning – the same thing urged me to go and do something to find out the culprits. MY wife understood my urgency and said to be careful. She knew me when I was serious about my work after the mantra effect made lot of changes in my behavior. I still not confided in her about the return of my mantra power .

Once in the Mumbai air port, I was taken by police car to spot of bomb blasts. By the time the bodies were removed and the injured taken to hospitals. I saw the debris strewn in all the directions and what remained once as platform 9 it looked like a junk yard with everything broken or out of original shape and form.

I was looking at every object lying there without knowing why? I went through the entire affected place and it took nearly two hours. Behind me the two commandos, the SP and Mumbai police officers were following me at a distance. I made a reverse trip looking more minutely by removing some thing here and something there- I did not what I was looking for but I was acting as per some command from me only and from where ? only Kali knew- I thought. After half an hour, while digging through the debris, I picked up a small iron plate without a shape-directly hit by the blast of the bombs- I looked at it for some time and told the SP to keep it in a bag. After ten minutes or so, I picked up a bunch of wires half burnt measuring a few inches at the most. I held them before me and fixed my eyes over them for a few minutes. Then I gave them to the SP for safe keeping. Thus within another two hours, I salvaged a few meaningless items which I handed over to the police officer.

I then went around the big station and saw all the places minutely. At the 2nd platform, I stopped to pick up a match box which contained a few unused sticks. I saw it closely and gave it to the SP. It took another two hours to make a microscopic inspection of all the platforms and outside the entrances also. In all I had collected twelve assorted items – having no meaning and relevance to the case from any point of view- which included me also.

I then asked the Mumbai police to take me to the DGP of Maharashtra police . I was greeted by the top official of the state who was with his deputies- looking worried more about the after effects of the killings by the bomb blasts than the loss of human lives. I told him to get forensic experts and a finger print specialists to help me. I then openly told that I was hungry and so also the SP and others who were with me when I was in the station for six to seven hours after landing at Mumbai air port. He felt sorry for not having extended the common courtesy

By the time I had my food and some rest, the experts I wanted arrived . I was taken to the forensic wing of a big building where I was taken inside - a spacious hall fully air conditioned. I was given a comfortable chair to sit and some snacks and water bottles. I told the Mumbai police that I needed privacy and only the experts and specialist should remain inside and others outside if they wanted. I told the group what I wanted and gave the twelve pieces which I picked up from the area of bomb blast.

They said they would take the items to the laboratory which was in the block next to the hall where I was seated. I said ok and they all left me alone to take rest which I took with the effect of mantra. I slept for quite some time peacefully- since I was wide awake throughout the night at my age of 68.

When I was woken up by one of the experts, I asked him whether the reports were ready. He gave a file in which there were many reports on those twelve items which ended with a report of the finger prints. They pointed out to be belonging to two humans only. About the items which were scrutinized the result was pointing to three special powerful RDX bombs- In the wires there were some marks of the manufacturer which pointed out to be from local shops. But the small plate used for fixing the bombs was from a number plate of a vehicle- only a part of engraved numbers – found out – with electronic microscope. The first was not completely damaged- in the next row- the remaining numbers were 6-89- the third and the fourth numbers were missing- the report elaborated that since the letters and numbers were engraved, the impressions remained clearly on the plate.

I told the Mumbai police Chief to verify the vehicles with the number plates starting from 89 under the sub-division of 6. It took half an hour for the computer at the traffic department fully automated to get the details I wanted. I was with the DGP when the list was brought. I sat at the end of the table and others occupied the other chairs with the DGP in his usual place.

I went through each one of the names again and again without myself knowing why I was doing leave alone others in the chamber. Suddenly I pointed my index finger and told the DGP to get hold of that person with the vehicle number 06-8911. The officers in the room were surprised and shocked and I repeated my request- but like an order. The DGP quickly recovered from the shock of my behavior and told the officers to go and bring the person pointed out by me.

I then told everybody to leave me alone except a sentry to help me to get some snacks and tea- I wanted to think. Actually I wanted to recover from the shock myself. I got what I wanted and enjoyed the tea and snacks and told the sentry to wait outside and come when I needed his help. He saluted and left. I slept for two hours when I was woken up by the DGP who told me that the person I wanted was waiting for me outside.

I told him to get him inside and he should be there when I talked to him. He said ok.

A middle aged person entered. I did not waste time to mesmerize him.

I asked him to tell about the car no MH-C-06-8911.

" it was my car. I sold it to my mechanic. " he said under the influence of the mantra – that meant that it was truth. I asked him to give the address of the mechanic. He gave it immediately. I thanked him and asked him to go to sleep at a corner. Then I asked the DGP to take me to the address and he did what I told him. We went by an ordinary vehicle neither police nor taxi with DGP in plain clothes and the vehicle was driven by a policeman. We reached the mechanic shed after one and half hours using the police authority wherever required without the red light etc. The beat police were informed to give way for the car all along the route.

Once at a distance I got down telling the DGP to wait patiently in the car. I walked the distance to the garage- a small one- with only one car could be taken for repair. I saw an old man with some tools in his hand and two boys were attending to some repair work independently . When the old man saw me I saw him and he was mesmerized immediately. I asked him to tell about the car No – I gave. I asked the two boys to go inside and sleep after hypnotizing them one by one. The old man said that his son purchased the car for some client who wanted an old car. It was repainted and the repairs were attended to in the garage before giving to the client. I asked him to give the name and address of the client. He thought for a while and said that only his son knew the dealings and the client. About the whereabouts of his son, he said that he had gone to buy some spares and would be back at any time. I asked to sleep along with the two boys and waited.

Fifteen minutes it took for the son to return in his moped. He got down and saw me and I saw him. There- he came under my influence and once I was sure- I asked about the client to whom he had sold the car no I gave. He did not hesitate. He said that they were staying in a lodge near a railway station when he went to collect the balance of the sale price of the car. He did not know whether they were there at that place.

I signaled the car and it came to garage. I told the mechanic to take us to the lodge. We went for a few kilometers inside small lanes and streets and the mechanic asked the driver to stop near a meat shop. He then got down and showed the lodge- an old dilapidated building –with shops at the ground floor and full of glass windows in the first floor- most of them closed at that time. I told the DGP to wait inside the car and took the mechanic to the lodge. The office was in the first floor. I he area was Muslim dominated one. At the entrance to the lodge a small desk was kept and a Muslim young man was sitting on the small stool talking to a cell phone. On seeing the mechanic who was also a Muslim- they both wished and our mechanic enquired about the people who were there in the double room and who purchased the car from him. I saw he was hesitating. I mesmerized him on the spot and asked him to tell about the people who stayed there and where they were now.

The receptionist without reacting told me that those people told him that they had come to do something; after they completed their job- they had left. I asked him whether they had given anything or left something behind. He said that they had not taken their Quran book by oversight. I asked him to give it to me . He opened a box under his feet and took out the book. I went through it page by page and I had the jackpot at the page no 155. There I had a group photo of a family and a young man standing behind the parents. I showed the photo to the receptionist and he said that only the young man came and stayed there. I told him to come with me to the waiting car and he did. I asked the DGP to take the mechanic and the receptionist to the HQ.

We landed there at the DGP office and I told the DGP to take them into custody as they were the prime witnesses for identifying the culprits. It was 10.30 pm . I felt hungry and told the DGP to get me something to eat. Then I showed him the photo and pointed out to the young person as the one who with the help of one more had planted bombs.

I took the good food brought from the top class hotel and after my hunger had gone, I told the DGP to give me some time to tell where the two were hiding either in the city or outside of it. The DGP was beyond words to express his surprise and shock over my getting very close to the culprits within 36 hours after the bomb blast resulting in a huge loss of lives.

I saw the photo for a long time closely as if I was compelled to do so by someone. I suddenly lost my consciousness and was looking at several weird things everywhere and after a few minutes, I was subconsciously I saw the face of the person in the photo. He was lying on a bed in a room and when I saw through the open window- I saw the name of a mobile shop in some language . Next to the shop, there was a temple – a small one and something again written in the same language. At that time I saw a bus moving across. I saw the name in English –Gujarat government transport corporation and the bus did not stop. When I was about to change the direction of the view, I saw the board of a bank at the end of the building. I saw the name of bank- Lakhpat branch- Morarji bhai road. Then there was blackout. I did not know where I was for a few seconds before getting back my senses to realize that I was in the discussion room of the DGP Mumbai.

I got up and opened the door and there several officers were waiting for me. I told them that I wanted to see the DGP immediately. I went inside the room and the door closed automatically behind me. Within a few minutes the DGP looking tensed came to me and stood near me. I asked him to take a seat near me. Then what happened was another strange thing- I was telling him without my own control about my seeing the young man lying on a bed in room – on the Morarji bhai road- opposite to the Bank's Lakpat branch. He immediately swung into action and the first information he shared with me was the place where I had seen the young man was the nearest point to the Runn of Kutch – which was the border of India and Pakistan- probably the culprits were waiting for their return journey to their motherland after killing so many innocent people.

He then asked me to come with him to his own room and there he asked my permission whether he should move the matter of arresting the two through the police of Gujarat or inform the Home department Delhi to do the job or send a team to that place and arrest the two under his own supervision. I asked him how far the place was from Mumbai and how long it would take for reaching the town. I told him that his replies were not suitable for a direct attack except by a special helicopter. He also said that a direction action was better and that too by going by a helicopter. That meant that the CM should be informed and his permission was obtained. I told him to take me to the CM and I would get the permission for the helicopter trip. In the meantime, I asked him to prepare the ground work for the arrest through his trusted officers. He hesitated for a second and said that he did not believe anyone except his own conscience in that most sensitive case.

We went to see the CM after the DGP told him about a serious matter he had to discuss with him about the bomb blast. The CM already under enormous pressure from all quarters thanked the DGP for the good news – when there was no news from the DGP except his request for an urgent meeting- and asked the DGP to come forthwith. We went there within half an hour with the siren blaring and the red light switched on the vehicle.

Inside the big palace like building, the CM took us to a private room in the first floor through a lift. There he closed his room and the DGP showed the photo and pointed out the youngman- saying that he was the culprit and he was at that moment in a town in Gujarat very near to the Pakistan border. He asked his permission to hire a helicopter to go to the town and arrest the two and bring them back to Mubai before morning. He was so happy – he immediately gave permission to the DGP who immediately asked his IG to proceed with the hire formalities and keep the aircraft ready within half an hour. The CM then saw me and I saw him. He was mesmerized and I told him to give his order in writing with date and time to DGP and then asked him to forget having seen us and talked to us. Then I asked him to go into deep sleep and we left the CM's residence with an instruction to the police guards not to disturb him up as per his(CM's) instructions.

We boarded the helicopter with two senior and ten plain clothes sharp shooters and the place had to be reached with two hours at the most. The IG explored the town for a landing site and found that there was one in the army campus. He contacted the western air command and requested for permission to land the helicopter carrying the DGP at Lakhpat army camp- who was on an official work. It took some time for getting the permission. The Colonel in charge of the army camp said that he would make enquires before allowing the DGP to leave the camp. I told the DGP to say ok. He said that to the colonel and we landed at 2 .30 am and the colonel was waiting for us. I saw him and he saw me and everything went on smoothly as per my wish. We all got into the military van and asked the driver to go to the Morarji bhai road and he did within half an hour.

At a distance from the room I saw in my subconscious vision, I got down and told everyone to wait and I walked slowly close to the side of the street till I reached the building opposite to the bank.. I looked up and saw an open window. I searched for the staircase but could not. I saw a man sleeping on a wooden plank in front of a close shop right under the room. I woke him up and mesmerized him instantly. He showed me the way behind the building to the first floor room. I took him along with me and asked him to tap the door. After a few repeated knocks a man opened the door and saw the familiar face and asked what he wanted and why he had woken him up at that time. I seized that opportunity and looked into half closed eyes and he came under my control without any difficulty. I asked him to wake up the other person also and bring him to door> he did and when he saw me and I saw him he too was under my mantra power.

Then I contacted the DGP to come in front of the building – situated in front of the bank on the opposite side. The military van was brought and without a protest or struggle the two were asked to get inside the van and I asked them to go into deep sleep. I then asked the two officers to go with the local man who helped me to search the entire room and bring what they could use as evidences. They went and returned almost after thirty minutes- carrying lot of things- a box- a cloth bag- some papers and many more belonging to the two. They were asked to seal the room with the materials they had been asked to bring along with them before leaving the Mumbai by me.

Once everyone boarded the van, it flew at top speed to the army camp where we all got down and the colonel who was made to sleep in the van was woken up by me . On seeing me and others he was blinking and I told him to go inside his quarters and sleep deeply. We all got into the helicopter with three new passengers and it took off with a noise which did not disturb the sleeping culprits.

The helicopter landed at Mumbai airport at 6.45 am. The IG who was in our team had already talked to the Mumbai police to keep a van ready for us. When I got into the DGP office it was 7. 55 am. The DGP was almost in tears when he told me that it was impossible for him even to believe that the culprits of a bomb blast case was solved within 48 hours and the culprits were arrested and brought to the police custody safely> he said that there were many bomb blasts and many hundreds were killed. Even then the cases were not closed as the culprits were not apprehended.

He contacted the CM and told him that the culprits were brought safely to Mumbai and the police officers were checking the evidences found in the room of the culprits and also verifying the finger prints with the twelve pieces having finger prints already with police. If that matched, that was the end of the case. That confirmation came after an hour making the DGP to get tensed beyond his limit. He was sweating and once the happy news was intimated to him by the experts, he literally lifted me in the air and shouted – long live Baba ram". I extricated from his emotional outbursts and told him not to call me baba as the name signified divine merchants – nothing to do with divinity. He apologized and told all the top officers that the Chennai savior had cracked the case within 48 hours. The SP who came with me and the commandos were so happy they started hugging me to the extent of choking.

The CM wanted to see me and so I was taken in the DGP official car to meet the CM . It was nothing short of a royal welcome for me and the DGP was blowing my trumpet by telling everything that happened from the time we took off from Mumbai till we returned. The news was officially announced to the medias and the CM's place was full of media crew demanding the full story as to how the case was solved within 48 hours which had never taken place in the annuls of bomb blasts in the country from the date of independence.

I told the CM and the DGP that if ever they wanted to do something in return for my help, they should send me back to Chennai in a helicopter as I was very interested to avoid unwanted publicity which would not be good for my future help for any one. They protested initially to remain in Mumbai for a thanks giving party and finally the same helicopter which took us to the gujartat was engaged for my secret trip to Chennai with the SP and the two commandos.

When I landed at Chennai air port it was 3 pm. At 12 noon I boarded the helicopter which halted at Bangalore for refueling when I was served lunch. At the Chennai air port what I wanted to avoid at Mumbai- was waiting for me in advance. The DGP with a big garland and others with flower bouquets welcomed me and they openly called me the unknown force in Tamil. The state ministers with their usual shawls greeted me telling that they represented the CM.

Finally I was allowed to get into the government car that took me to my flat which I left exactly 48 hours before.

My wife and family members welcomed me and told me that according to the medias- I had cracked the impossible bomb blast case with a record time of 48 hours with an unimaginable speed and accuracy which no human possessed till now. The media reports confirmed that I should be rightly called the unknown force. I wanted to avoid publicity for me when the actual force which deserved the praise was the Kali and the mantra only. I felt awkward when I was praised for what was done through me by an unknown force. In the bomb case, right under consciousness I was going out of my control when I was seeing things after my unconsciousness.

I asked my wife to allow me to sleep till the next morning without any disturbance.

I took complete rest for five days by going to Bangalore with my wife where I had my own single bed room flat at Yeshwantpur. We both remained together without disturbance, going around Malleshwaram and avenue road. The climate was good and I got what I wanted –complete rest-eating and sleeping. No phone calls or guests or reporters etc. I felt that the real force which should be disturbed remained unidentified and I was subjected to interviews, press meetings etc.

My son and his wife who were with us at Chennai were pestered to get the whereabouts about me. Even the CM and the DGP asked for our contact details. My son told them that I wanted to take rest for a few days and hence I had gone to some religious place with my wife and would be back at the end of the week.

On Monday at 10 am I rang up the DGP's personal mobile number and told him that he should arrange for a secret meeting at some undisturbed place. He should invite on my behalf the Chief Justice of Chennai, Advocate general, the four lawyers and , the Chief Minister. He said that he would take care of the arrangements immediately. I had my morning food and was taking rest on the swing when the DGP told me that the meeting was arranged at 4 pm behind the Police HQ- at the place where I was kept by the police after my arrest. He told me that it was meant for top secret meetings and it was converted for my stay when I had to be given top the highest security as per the CM's direction.

He told me that a police vehicle would come and pick me up at 3.15 pm from my flat.

The meeting was attended by all the special invitees, without fail except one lawyer who was away to London on a case. He was a barrister also. I entered the familiar hall but totally transformed into a business meeting place- a long table-with six chairs on either side and in the centre there was a chair for the chairperson of the meeting- with bottle water etc.

I was guided by the DGP to take the centre chair but I told him that only the CM should sit there. But the CM sat on the first chair on the right side and insisted on my taking the centre chair as the meeting was called by me only. I thanked all those who were present and to cut the formal talk, I straightaway plunged into the purpose of the secret meeting.

" Respected Chief Minister The DGP, The chief Justice of high court, the advocate general and my lawyer friends- almost the medias has categorically confirmed me as the unknown force and the latest bomb blast case had given them additional evidence about my status. I neither deny nor accept that I am the unknown force- but the fact remained that the force is acting through me which cannot be denied.

Now the reason for this secret meeting is –simple. To hand over the self confessed list of properties, cash jewellery and other forms of assets belonging to the persons punished by the unknown force directly till now to the Chief minister in your presence. I want to make it clear that it is the will of the unknown force that every paisa of this confiscated wealth should be spent for the people starting from the bottom line of the society. There should be no wastages, misappropriation or frauds in using this enormous amount under any circumstances. Those who are present should be in the team to manage the funds for the public welfare to the last rupee. I further request the CM to add the ill-gotten wealth seized from the 4879 criminals who confessed and furnished the list of their ill-gotten wealth giving the details where they had hidden or stored and in what forms. The amount invested in foreign banks and properties should be disposed off by moving the appropriate authorities of the central government. All the landed assets and jewellery should be sold in public auctions under my personal supervision and the proceeds should be kept in all the nationalized banks at the district HQ branches of the state.

Once the phase one of the operation –PUBLIC WELFARE- is over-that is converting the assets into liquid form- then it should be apportioned as per the list of priorities prepared by me but subject to your approval.

to provide medical facilities matching super specialty private hospitals in all government medical centres from the general hospitals to the Primary health centres at the villages

to provide uninterrupted electricity supply to all the villages first and then upwards to the city at a concessional rate to be fixed by you all. There should be no electricity supply for cinema theatres, cricket matches, clubs, TV stations- star hotels and race courses, big shopping malls .It for them to produce the electricity they wanted by using heavy duty generators which are available in the market. The middle class and lower class consumers should be given maximum subsidy by the government while the high class people should be charged to the maximum possible . If there is any protest whether organized in public or in the courts, announce that I will be representing the government to face them

to provide potable-treated water free for everyone one in the state and the sale of bottled water in any form should be banned. . If there is any protest whether organized in public or in the courts, announce that I will be representing the government to face them

to establish Public distribution ration shops in every village and in other places a ration shop for every 1000 card holders

to provide gas cylinders at a fixed highly subsidized price to the lower middle and lower class people and at the actual cost for the middle class and the cost plus to the upper class to cover the loss in the total distribution

rationing the supply of petrol for unnecessary consumers like the children college students, and fat rich people who simply waste the imported fuel for fun and personal pleasure trips. . If there is any protest whether organized in public or in the courts, announce that I will be representing the government to face them

To buy the maximum number of latest model buses and ply them in all the routes in the state to stop the foot board travel and standing passengers within the next one year.

To lay the cement road in all the villages, towns and slum areas in the city and provide 6 lanes highways between all the district HQ to the state capital and asphalted roads to all the villages

Stop the sale of liquors in the state forthwith including the supply to the star hotels and elites and if any one files any case in the courts, I will take represent the government

Bring all the educational institutions from the primary school level to that of the deemed university under the state control and ownership- banning private ownership in the field of education in the state. If there is any protest whether organized in public or in the courts, announce that I will be representing the government to face them

I then gave the lists I brought to all those who were present and asked for their views. As expected by me, they were one in welcoming my suggestions which they said were aimed at removing all most all the problems faced by the public now.

I thanked them and took out the 23 original confession notes which I had brought from Tihar jail and gave them to the Chief Justice and requested him to hand over them to the Chief Justice of India without involving me in the process. He accepted the plastic cover containing the notes and promised to carry out the order immediately.

I told them that I should not be disturbed any further in any manner as I wanted to enjoy my retired life. I made it clear that I did want any special favours for me or for my family members. I should not be invited for any government or private functions and no awards or cash or properties will be accepted by me. What I have done was done by the unknown force through me and I did nothing personally and hence does not deserve any praise or compensation for my involvement.

If at all you show your respect to me and my missions so far, please act as per my list of public welfare schemes without worrying about any type of interventions from any quarters. I will be there without your request or call at all those places where I feel my presence is necessary - to help you to carry out the welfare measures. Give wide publicity that the unknown force is behind all the public welfare activities and any one opposes them would be treated as public enemy-one- and would be punished accordingly then and there. Remember - no force on earth can stop you from accomplishing the public services in any manner. You have the support of the unknown force –whether it would act through me or any one of you- for a change. Good Luck and unknown force would bless you all"

I shook hands with each one of them and bade them good bye. Without turning my back I left the room and the police HQ and boarded the bus which stopped for signal at a junction and reached my flat through a circuitous route.

I started my routine life as usual